INSANITY

A Girl I Used To Know

D'MYA J. SMITH

Foreword: Kiara A. Johns
Editor: Sundra Hilsinger

ISBN: 978-1-7341948-1-4

First Edition

Preeminent Publishing Co.
www.DmyaJSmith.com

Printed in the United States of America.

Cover Design by 100Covers.com
Interior Design by FormattedBooks.com

TABLE OF CONTENTS

DEDICATION

This book is dedicated to April McCullum; God ALWAYS sends His angels. They are real, and they are beautiful.

A THOUGHT FOR READERS

I have found that being insane is quite fulfilling. We all know the basic definition: "Doing the same thing over and over expecting a different result." That sounds abnormal, right? Sane, meaning "healthy" from the Latin adjective sanus, is a goal in everyone's life, right? What if we have misrepresented the meaning? What if the people we call crazy were not expecting the same results? Maybe their objective was to build strength or even numbness. Maybe strength and being numb are possibly one in the same. And I bet if I keep talking, keep digging, and keep searching, I will find insanity is a common thing. Funny how perception, experience, and the use of words works.

A NOTE TO READERS

Do not let anyone call you anything other than your name. Your past does not consume you; it is a tool meant to lead you. You owe it to yourself, your purpose, and to God to acknowledge and rejoice over your testimony. If anyone hasn't told you today, I love you. I love you, and I'm glad you're still here; REJOICE, you made it another day.

And not only so, but we glory in tribulations also: knowing that tribulation worketh patience; And patience, experience; and experience, hope:And hope maketh not ashamed; because the love of God is shed abroad in our hearts by the Holy Ghost which is given unto us. Romans 5:3-5 KJV

This confidence in God, this faith, and dedication is my new form of insanity, and I have never felt saner

FOREWORD BY KIARA A. JOHNS

Perhaps I was born this way, or maybe it was my environment that shaped my perception of what life is and has the potential to be. I've always fought with two voices, wishing that I knew for certain I'd obey the one that encourages me to do right. Indeed a battle of my conscience mind and my will to exist in a different waythan what I've always known. I have always questioned whether sanity was something that everyone fought to maintain and aspired to keep. Honestly, there seems to be an element of freedom for those who have completely relinquished thecares and holds of what society considers to be normal; after all, what exactly is normal? For many, all we have ever wanted was to be free to exist and protected ina world of grave uncertainty and dangers unaware. Yet, as I reflect on my life, and the lives of many of my peers, it seems as if we live in a world where everyone is struggling to hold on to their portion of sanity, fighting for their natural human rights in hopes of finding protection in a society that wasn't created to serve us. A society that never meant to allow us to be normal. I am no stranger to the struggle of maintaining mental health. For years I've dealt with post-traumatic stress disorder. In fact, trauma had a reoccurring role in my life, rearing its ugly head in many different facets. As I read Insanity, a Girl I Usedto Know with a heavy heart, I smiled as D'Mya shared a truth, a struggle that so many men and women alike have fought. She shares the trauma that comes from incest, molestations, alcohol abuse, and self-mutilation. She dives into the depths of chaos that trauma causes as it pertains to building healthy relationships and self-esteem. Upon meeting D'Mya in 2013, I remember my mother sharing that one of the ladies of Victory House reminded her so much of me; to which at the time, I politely smirked and thought to myself 'impossible, nobody is like me, because nobody knows the pain I've been through or the mistakes I've made; nobody has the same fight and drive as me.' As D'Mya and I began to engage, I slowly but surely understood from which paradigm my mother viewed our similarities. However, it wasn't until I read this book that I understood the depths of D'Mya's struggles and her courage to overcome adversity. She tells a story that many are not brave enough to share, and that some minds and spirits aren't big enough to comprehend. Over the years, I have watched D'Mya grow into an amazing young woman, one who is confident and charismatic. A woman who speaks up and works to defend the rights of others, knowing all too well what it feels like to be overlooked and for her truth to be rejected—because of its inconvenience. Yet, somehow she musters the courage to motivate others and continuously fight for a better life and relationship with God. She is a living testimony of what prayer, faith, and successfully working to maintain your mental health looks like; Or as she would say, "A few milligrams and a whole lot of Jesus." In more recent years, it seems as though it is becoming the norm to make mental health and self-preservation a priority. We, the millennial generation, are often vocal about enrolling in therapy, seeking life coaches, and actively searching for ways to decompress. Perhaps we will be the generation to break the stigma surrounding mental health and abuse. Moreover, it is apparent throughout this body of work, by her transparency, D'Mya is committed to doing her part to encourage others to seek treatment and find healing from past traumas.

I believe everything happens for a reason, so when you corrupt something, you have not only taken a sense of peace; you've created a monster.

Chapter One

BABY GENIUS

"STOP," I heard my mom scream from the next room.

She and Grandpa must have been playing tag again- it was always loud when they did. Last time they played tag, my grandfather grabbed my mother by the hair and took her into his room. He always said she plays hard to get but that he loves chasing her. My mother's hair was all down the hall. I missed her long pretty hair.

I heard another scream; I didn't know why he always followed her. She needed a break from playing.

Jerrod reached over quickly to cover my ears. He was the best big brother ever.

"It's okay, Janee," he said. "Everything is okay- don't be afraid."

I glanced at him in confusion and asked, "Why would I be scared, Jerrod?"

Stunned, he stared at me.

"I can't be afraid of what happens all the time. That would make me crazy. C-R-A-Z-Y," I finished.

Laughing a little, "Why do you know how to spell crazy? Who taught you that?" he asked.

"I sounded it out. I hear mommy saying it all the time, then when she sees me listening, she hehes and pinches my face after calling me crazy."

Laughing, "I can't believe you know how to spell and say all this stuff at two years old. You are so smart."

I smiled and pinched his face.

Walking into the front room where Jerrod and I were, my grandmother smiled at us. "That's right. You're our little crazy, silly girl," she said, pinching my face like Mommy did.

I had to look at my grandma. Why didn't Grandpa ever play tag with her? She moved when he came into any room, and she was always quiet around him. Maybe he'd put her on punishment again. Before punishment, Grandpa always gave her a whooping. I didn't like whoopings at all- I always got my toys taken away right after.

"Jerrod," called my grandfather.

Before getting up, my brother let out a weird noise, then quickly stood and went to my grandfather. Jerrod was also a good boy, he never made Grandpa wait. He said he was too scared to. His eyes looked like water every time Grandpa called his name- I didn't know why he had wet eyes, it's not like he ever got a whooping.

"Nae Nae, let's watch a movie!" said my grandma.

Excited, I asked, "Can we watch Pooh?"

"Yes, we can watch *Winnie the Pooh.*"

I had what Grandmother calls, a small bladder. She said I peed like a horse, but I didn't look like a horse. She confused me a lot. I always had to pee, especially during movies.

Grandma let me get up on my own to go to the bathroom. As I walked down the short hallway, I turned to my left (I always used my hands to help me with directions), and faced the bathroom. Before walking in, I saw Grandpa and Jerrod playing. I thought *it must be time for bed*, because at bedtime, Grandpa always called Jerrod into the bathroom for a bath, I think. He grabbed this box with a blue top and a word on it spelled V-A-S-E-L-I-N-E. I thought it must be lotion in a vase, like the thing that keeps flowers. Grandpa always lotioned himself and then Jerrod. Jerrod must have had a dry butt because Grandpa always paid special attention to it. Maybe that's why he never got whoopings.

Grabbing me, "Janee, I'll let you use the big girl bathroom. My bathroom," Grandma said, pulling me away."

I smiled, "Really!" I said jumping up and down.

I fell asleep before I could ask Jerrod how his bath was, and Mommy was too busy laying in our bed, waiting to be tucked in. Grandpa loved her the most.

It seemed like a few minutes later I woke up to the sound of sniffling-someone must have had a cold. Walking towards the big room with a couch, I stopped to see my mom looking out the window. She must have been wishing again.

"Shanelle, I can't take this shit anymore," she said. "He's starting with my kids too, saying he wants to keep after them and shit. You know what that means. I can't anymore."

Ooooo Grandpa is gonna whip her if he hears her, I thought. I tiptoed back into bed before anyone heard me.

A few days later I found out that my mom had left, but I didn't mind because Jerrod and I got time with Shanelle, my mom's best friend. But Shanelle told us we had to leave soon. So, a few hours later she called the men with uniforms and they took us.

After a few months, I found myself back with my brother and his great-aunt Ruth. It had seemed like forever since I was able to play with Jerrod, and his Auntie loved me so much that she even called me her niece. This was nice after the other four homes.

I had a lot of stuffed animals, but the smiles were too nice. They could frown sometimes. Auntie always got us snacks and we had movie nights. It was great to not hear screaming anymore. Jerrod and I went on adventures. He knew I hated the grass, so he put a tent in the African room, with African print sheets, jungle cat decorations and showed me a secret. He didn't make me touch it, so I was ok with it. I didn't have anything to show him, so we went into the kitchen and Auntie shouted, "Plates made for dinner." It was spaghetti, and the noodles were light pink. We ate, laughed, and were happy. I didn't feel so C-R-A-Z-Y after all.

Chapter Two

THIS IS WHAT "FAMILY" IS ALL ABOUT

Part 1: Love at First Sight

I was sitting down in what seemed like an adult room. It seemed that way to me because there was a table with a computer and many papers. No kid has writing paper without colors, where were the pretty pictures? I jumped a little when my observations were interrupted by the doorknob turning.

"Hi, sweetie," greeted Miss Carrie, my longtime friend. "Remember when I said I have a few people for you to meet? I mentioned it at our last visit in Livonia," she continued.

"Yes," I replied.

"Well honey, they are here to meet you," she squeaked with excitement. "We found your blood relatives to take you home, honey."

I loved meeting new people; I knew I should've drawn a picture for them before I came.

"Miss Carrie?" I said, hopefully. "Do I have time to make them a picture before we meet?"

"Not this time, they are right outside," she said. Calling towards the hallway, "You guys can come on in!"

My eyes widened.

Three people came in, and I saw that I was right about the room because they were all grown-ups. Two were boys, and one was a girl. The girl had pretty black hair, and her skin looked very much like a marshmallow, very white. The one boy was a brown shade that I would probably have to mix in my coloring box to make the right color. His gray hair came in before the others', I guessed. And the other boy was the exact color of my brown crayon; his pictures would probably be the best. He looked younger than the others; maybe they were his parents.

"Janee, these are the Dukes," Miss Carrie announced.

I guessed adults were like robots, they all smiled at the same time, and in the same way; right at me.

They quickly introduced themselves. The perfect brown was my dad, the gray-haired man was my grandpa (I would call him papa), and the marshmallow woman was my grandma.

A few days later, I packed all my toys and new pencils, and Miss Carrie helped me load them into the car, where the Dukes were waiting. I jumped in, and they started the engine.

My new home was pretty. I had a yellow room with one wall covered in red sponge spots. I overheard Papa say that we lived in a city called West Bloomfield; everything was pretty there. I wondered who colored the city; I hoped to be that good one day.

My grandparents bought me new toys and hats that had dresses to match. Grandmother said I needed the dresses for church. Well, not church, they called it "The Hall."

The Kingdom Hall had pretty pictures, and the big people always came to kiss my cheeks. They were kind and always gave me candy, too. We sang songs and spoke about "armodedon." Later, Grandma corrected me and said it was Armageddon. She said we had to follow Jehovah's wishes, so we don't miss the tea party. If we didn't follow Jehovah's wishes, we wouldn't be covered and make it to paradise. I hoped I was at the tea party. I had already picked out my dress and favorite doll.

My grandma also explained to me how she was not only my grandma but that she was my dad's grandma as well- she said that she is my great grandmother. I had a lot of grandmothers, my great-grandmother's name was María, her mother's name was Marisol, and Dad's mother's name was Cynthia. Sometimes Grandma María told me a little about my mom's parents when I asked. Their names were Luke and Carol. I hadn't seen them in a while.

"Janee," Papa called.

"Yes, papa?"

"Ready for our cheese and crackers?" he asked.

Papa and I would have our cheese and crackers almost every day; it was our time, even Grandma never came in. He read a story and we sat and laughed while eating. Papa was my best friend.

"I think it's time for you to have a friend, huh?" he said.

I stared at him blankly and responded, "You are my friend, Papa."

"Aw sweetie," he chuckled, "I sure am. But I was talking about someone closer to your age."

"Oh. Could they see my dolls?" he nodded. "I would like that very much," I replied.

"Great, I have someone for you to meet tonight at bible study," he said.

After the hall, Grandmother introduced me to a girl named Kimmy, who said she would be my friend; therefore, we arranged a sleepover. My first sleepover ever!

That Friday, we played restaurant. We had Grandma and Papa sit down at the made-up table and took their order. We did so well that they actually paid us! Soon after, we pulled out our dolls. Kimmy had everything. Sometimes I wished she'd forget a few things. We played house and I was so happy to have a friend, even though she was three years older than me. She cared a lot.

"Janee and Kimmy," Grandma called, "it's time to come from the back porch! You two have to take a bath and get ready for bed."

"Ok," we called in unison.

"Aw," I sighed.

"It's okay, Janee; the night is not over," I looked up at her. "We can continue playing house in your room."

My face brightened, "really!"

"Yes," she responded. "Come on, let's hurry up."

After our baths, Grandma said our nightly prayer and tucked us in. I was hoping to play house, but we had left all the dolls on the back porch, so I closed my eyes and prepared to sleep. Shortly after, I felt something wet on my neck.

"Ew," I giggled. It was Kimmy kissing my neck.

"Hush," she shushed.

"What are you doing?" I giggled once more. "You are kissing me, you must love me. Grandma says kisses mean love," I explained.

"Yes, I do love you," she said.

Next, I felt my night gown lifting up; I squirmed a little.

"Wait, wait, wait," she explained. "This means I really love you."

She continued lifting my gown up and pulled my panties down.

"Lay on your back," she told me. "I'm your best friend; this is what best friends do."

I laid on my back. She then got on top of me. Her hands touched my chest, and she started making weird noises as she rubbed against me. A few minutes later, I felt a weird feeling on my private area which Grandma called my chicken, then she stopped. She got off of me and told me she loved me and how she loved being there.

"But you can't tell anyone," she explained. "Best friends don't tell things they do with each other."

I nodded my head and smiled.

"Let's go to sleep now. We will have time for more secrets tomorrow."

Two days later.

"Get up baby," my dad called, waking me up. "Get ready, you're spending the day with me."

I loved spending time with Dad. He almost always had me by his side. All his friends knew and loved me; they always said I was so cute. My uncle Devin was around a lot too; he said I was just like his baby. Dad even helped me with reflection contests, which were art contests in elementary school. From digital art, to clay, all the way to paintings. That year I drew my own community and won second place. My community included the diversity in my family, since I am of Hispanic and African American decent. Two days before that, I'd won the first-place award in the kindergarten spelling bee, and my clay butterfly was put on display. Grandma always took special care of my awards, and Papa bragged about me to everyone else in the family.

I had much to be proud of until I slipped up.

"Hello," my grandma said, answering the phone.

"Hello, Mrs. Dukes, this is Principal Charlotte Chrismon of Creekwood Elementary," Mrs. Chrismon announced.

"How are you?" my grandmother asked.

"I'm doing well, ma'am. I'm calling in regards to your granddaughter."

"Well, is she alright?"

"She is just fine. An altercation occurred this morning. Her Kindergarten teacher, Mrs. Marx, informed Janee that she could not play at recess."

"Well, why couldn't she play during recess?"

"She withdrew herself from a group project, and in return, she kicked Mrs. Marx."

"No, she did not! My husband and I are on the way."

Getting in trouble was something that happened a lot. That was not the first time either; the first time was in preschool. I had to bite this girl because she wouldn't get out of my tent. It was her fault!

Three years later.

Grandma wished me a merry happy day today. I wasn't sure what today was, but I guessed it's what the worldly people called a "birthday." Grandma said we couldn't celebrate birthdays because of what happened to John the Baptizer when he went to that party; I was still confused as to how a celebration pertained to that, but I guessed it was Jehovah's will. Instead, she would take me shopping the day after my birthday and Christmas.

We did have winter and fall dinners, and she'd invite the family over every time I won an art contest at school and for each talent show. Grandma María made sure I was involved in almost everything at school. The school bragged about my talents to her, even with all the suspensions mixed in between. If I was so great, how in the world did they end up naming me, Insanity? Grandma would say, "All these rewards mean nothing when you're bad." I tried to do better, but people were mean. I always complained about having no friends, but then things just got worse.

Part 2: Cousins, a Kid's First Best, Well, Everything

"Dad, is Janee staying the night?" my cousin Ken asked. My great-grandmother had two children, my uncle Steven and my grandmother Cynthia.

My great uncle Steven had five sons, Ken, Josh, Brandon, Roger, and Sean, but Sean had died years ago in a car crash.

"If she wants to, Ken, it's fine with me," responded my uncle.

"Stay, Janee. You can stay up and play video games and eat snacks with Josh and I."

"Okay, I'll stay," I responded in excitement.

I didn't have any friends, and Grandmother didn't allow me to stay the night at anyone's house except my brother's occasionally.

"Josh, is Mom and Dad asleep?" Ken asked.

"I don't know. Why?"

"Because I want to get some snacks from the stash and don't want them to know. Duh, dumb ass."

"I can go check."

Josh walked up the stairs.

"What level is that, Ken?" I asked. I never really understood video games. I only liked playing Pokémon.

"There really aren't any levels, but I'm kicking this guy's ass. Soulcalibur is the shiiiiit."

"Hey, Ken. They are asleep." Josh said, returning downstairs.

Mark paused the game and turned to face Josh and me.

He looked at me. "Janee, want me to show you something cool that I taught Josh?"

Josh turned his head to me quickly and then looked away.

"Yeah!" I said, wanting badly to belong.

"Okay, but you have to swear to do everything I say and not tell anyone because it's a cousin thing, okay?" I nodded.

Ken began pulling down my lime green sweatpants. I squirmed out of confusion.

"Be still," he demanded.

He continued.

"OUCH," I flinched.

"SHHH, you have to be quiet and still remember?" I glanced over and saw Josh watching.

"Okay," I said.

"After this, you will be officially a part of the family! We will always have your back. No more foster homes like before," he whispered as he pulled down his shorts.

"You like that, don't you," he said in my ear.

I said nothing but jumped.

"Stay still, I'm almost done."

Well apparently, that wasn't and wouldn't be the last time I'd stay still.

"Janee," my grandmother called.

"Yes, G?" I answered.

"I invited Ken and Josh over to keep you company while we all go to the Marisol's wedding."

"Okay. Can we get some snacks before you guys leave, too?"

"Of course, dear."

I enjoyed having my cousins over. I loved being close to them. Sometimes we would fight, and at times they would punch or slap me, but I knew that was because I had bonded with them and they were treating me like a friend.

"Okay, the coast is clear," Josh said as he walked away from the window, checking to see if the adults had left.

"Good," Ken responded with a smirk. "Now this time, we are going to do something different," he paused. "Josh, I want you to show Janee what I taught you, and then I'm going to show you what I've been teaching Josh so you can get the real feel," Josh nodded his head in agreement.

"So, both of you are teaching this time?" I asked to find certainty.

"Yes, now it's time to get started," said Ken eagerly.

I'd felt this close to people before. Like when my grandfather on my mom's side would place me on his lap. He always told me how good I made him feel and how that made him happy. His wife, my grandmother, would be so proud of me too. After I made Grandfather Luke happy, Grandma would take me straight to Toys R Us and buy me five new toys before taking me home. They had to have loved me, they always told me I was just as good as my mom. Grandma Cynthia let me visit Luke and Carol from time to time, but it wasn't often. They'd come around, tell me I was a good girl, buy me presents, and then take me home, but I was not allowed to spend the night at their house, and I wondered why; they were my family, what's so different from my other sleepovers?

Sleepovers became my favorite thing to do. To be in the midst of other people around my age gave me an unexplainable high. That's why I was so happy when Grandma told me that I could start spending the night at Kimmy's grandmother's house.

"So, you know how we play house?" Kimmy asl

"Yes, yes, yes!" I squeaked.

"Well, Kelz is going to play too."

Kelz was her brother. He was one year young He was like Josh, playing dolls with us and tri Grandma called him a "gentleman."

"Ok," I said. "I like when we can all play together."

I soon after found out that Kimmy and Ken were very close. They went to the same school and were really good friends. I was so happy Ken was letting me be friends with her too.

As time went on, most of the time, I only played house with Kelz. We liked each other, so we had to be quiet about everything. Kimmy was even nice enough to not tell anyone, and she was allowed to join whenever she wanted. We were all so close! They were like my long-lost cousins; we were all best friends.

This isn't a sad story; this is only clarity, nothing to be surprised nor offended by; it's only here to make sense. I am for everyone, but I belong to no one. I stick to the facts.

Part 3: Welcome the Voices

Five years later.

"Janee, go to your room!" my father commanded.

"No, I don't have to!" I screamed. "I am not a boy. You can't push me around like one."

"Get your ass in your room," he said after raising his hand to me.

I immediately shot back, "Leave me alone!"

"I'm sending you to Carol and Luke's house, and you know what they're about. Sure, you'll have whatever you want, but you'll also be trapped! Is that what you want?" he yelled.

I began tearing up, my feet buried in the ground, not even a sway in my arms; I was paralyzed.

"You're too big, and you need to keep your hair up. Maybe they can help you there," he finished.

dy reconnected, and I rushed into my room, grabbing my favorite notebook filled with my writings. The tears rolled down my face, ping my neck all the way down my chest. I began to write:

You broke my heart.
You made me feel ugly.
You have no respect for me.
You only think about yourself.
You threatened to send me to a home that would not be safe and that I could not escape.
You never came to any of my graduations and other special days.
Dad, you don't even know my birthday; that really makes me sad.
You never said, "I'm proud of you."
You only said I was bad.
My attitude reflects my surroundings.
I wish you knew what was true.
This family is misleading you.
I tried to tell you, but all you said was leave.
You're very selfish, Dad, I hate you in many ways.
I do still love you, Dad, and I pray for you every day.
Though you don't like me, Dad, I still pray and pray.
But until you change and love me the same, you are awarded
World's Worst Dad.

Two weeks later, I found out he was previously diagnosed with paranoid schizophrenia.

"Ahhh, isolation." I let out, throwing my bags on the bed, just getting home from school. My heart was heavy, and I didn't know why. There was a *Proud Family* marathon today, and I expected to be all in.

Yesterday, my grandma almost caught Ken and me. Even after all these years, we were still at it. The funny thing is, we bickered and argued all the time but did everything together. I got along better with Josh; he was also gentler. Every time I did it now though something felt so wrong, it hurt every time. I didn't always want it; had I ever? My heart ached.

"*Aren't you on duty*?" the voices began.

The voices grew louder and louder; it's better when you don't fight it.

"*Unconditional love, this is the way to prove it*," the voices continued.

My Uncle Steven's voice popped up. Could it have been his voice all along? "*You can't rape the willing.*"

"*Who, who could ever want you?*" the voices again.

I pleaded with my mind to block them; begged to hear myself for once.

"*You have been doing the same things for years. How dare you act like it's bringing you any pain?*" the voices screamed.

I caved in; I kept trying to explain that I had no clue why I wanted to feel so much; I began to answer the voices. "Feelings always keep people coming; they may leave, but they are always there."

"*You asked for the* 'pain' *that is inflicted upon you,*" the voices answered.

"I just..." I started to answer.

"Janee," My grandmother called, interrupting my conversation.

I turned around to face her. "You can't stay here if you get pregnant," she said before walking out.

"*Time to cut again,*" the voices demand. "*Cutting demands feelings, isn't that what you want?*"

"But I feel nothing when I cut," I answered.

"*Just pitiful. They call you insane for a reason. The only time you're not crazy is when you're pleasuring,*" the voice said. "*Which will you choose this round, back or knees?*"

"I do it because I love them," I said.

The voices answered, "*That's why they call you a pro. Better hurry up before they don't want you again. You love them, right?*"

I had heard about this word love before. I had even heard about sex. Love was always explained by a feeling, a strong urge for affection with hearts and ribbons. While the word sex was described in a hush. Some said the two are completely different, and others said they go hand in hand.

The next day, I sat in Clarksville Middle School digging for an answer after my friend, Ryan, had asked a question.

"What's your body count?" Ryan asked.

I looked up in a daze. Finally, I blurted out, "Huh? What are you talking about?"

He chuckled. "How many people have you had sexual relations with?"

"What are you, Planned Parenthood?" I responded, hoping to deter him from the subject.

"Answer me. You're real, right?" he pressured, smiling.

Clearing my throat, "Well, at two, there was one; by five, there was two; I am twelve now, and there since has been three. I have loved six people."

Thank God I was taught how to love at a young age. I showered people with affection every time I saw them, and I always put others before myself. Things worked best when I did, especially when I put people before myself; I made sure to do my absolute best when it came to my family. I was rewarded for good behavior. They spoke more calmly, and overall, everyone was in a better mood.

I had loved my mother's father ever since I could remember. When I was younger, it would be just him and me until my mother, grandmother, and brother, Jerrod, came back from school or work. My grandfather always played my favorite *Winnie the Pooh* movie and cooked me either shrimp or steak- my favorites.

As I think back, at times, it hurt loving him; however, Jerrod always said loving my grandfather was okay because Grandpa made it easier. Grandpa kept a special oil for Jerrod in the bathroom ready for use. At least, I thought it was special until two years ago when I realized it was only Vaseline.

When my mother loved my grandpa, she was used to it. She didn't squirm like Jerrod and I; Jerrod hadn't loved Grandpa in years; maybe that was one thing Jerrod couldn't do right. I assumed that as much as my mother used to love my grandfather, he must've been her first love. Unfortunately, I never saw Grandma and Grandpa loving each other. Grandpa always said she never did it right. I'd seen my grandparents from time to time since moving in with Great Grandmother, María, seven years before. The loving still hasn't stopped. He still played the same movie, cooked the same meal, and he even took me shopping. I loved him as I always had, and I didn't squirm as much either.

The voices had arrived.

"*All this talking, and you forgot the others; how does it feel to be the family toy?*" they questioned.

"It makes me feel wanted," I said.

"*Oooohhh but not loved?*"

"Love deals with pleasure, so I guess I did feel loved. I didn't ever hear the word insanity."

"*Yeah, yeah, yeah, but you know they don't have to repeat what you already know.*"

"You're right," I replied. "But my cousins are on their way, so I have to go."

The voices chuckled, "*Better hurry up. You have a lot of work to do.*"

After my job was over, I did my routine prayer. I pleaded, begged, bribed, and cried for God to block any pregnancies associated with my acts. I also begged Him to keep new acts in secrecy to avoid ridicule from the adults of the family. Although they knew how I loved my cousins, they still continued to call me names. It seemed like their favorite word to call me was crazy. They must have been right because I started to hear myself less and less.

The voices reached out to me. "*Why do you do what you do? You pull from pain to love; it can't be both.*"

I answered, "Maybe to prove I am worthy."

"*Or how about: maybe you're a whore,*" they replied.

Closing my eyes, "Or maybe I just want to be good at something."

Chapter Three

COMFORT UNDERNEATH THE PAIN

R. I. P. (7th grade, 3:20 a.m.)

Remember that sweet innocent girl?
I do
She always wore a smile and greeted everyone she met, and only
whippings made her upset
She did nothing but kind things for others, except when she slept
She dreamed of happiness and her future success
She was the kindest, sweetest girl I ever met
Too bad she's gone and may not ever come back
"What happened?" you may ask
Well let me reflect
Her mother left her (and her brother)
She wonders if she ever looked back
She wonders where her mother is,

and if she'll ever come back
She hopes she's okay,
and that her past isn't bothering her
like an itch or a gnat
Foster home to foster home
Will there be a home for her at last?
She lives with her great grandmother now
She started out nice,
but now everything ends with a fight
She doesn't treat her right
She just wants to fight and fight
She wants to run away from her life,
but she has nowhere to hide
Someone always finds her
She wants someone to save her
before time runs out
Tick, Tick
Time is running out for her
Who will be the one to save her?
She has been mentally and physically taken away from
She wishes she could talk to her grandparents about her mother,
but that privilege has been taken away
because of the last four-hour stay
It was gone again; her grandfather took it away
She watched her grandmother close the door on her regained innocence
It's gone now, and she wants it back
But it's gone
Taken too many times
It was not fair to her
She never had the choice,
or the control, not even the help
Innocence was not accessible to her
She had to be played with
Her innocence is gone,
physically and mentally, or did it ever exist?
Her thoughts have turned into negativity,
Her love into hate,

Her strength into weakness,
Her heart is gone,
She doesn't feel she is loved by anyone
She hates herself,
She doesn't want to live
ssshhluck, ssshhluck
A blade slides across her wrist
ssshhluck, ssshhluck
She's bleeding inside and out
ssshhluck, ssshhluck
Her so-called family cuts deep into her heart
ssshhluckkkk
She's scarred for life
I just hope they don't cut deep enough into her soul to kill her hopes and promises for herself
Time is running out
Shhh...
Listen, her heart is beating,
slower and slower,
she's almost gone.
May you Rest in Peace, Janee S. Dukes.

"Did I do it?"

"*Do what?*" the voices answered.

"Master death."

"*Haha, GET UP! It'll be time to go back down later.*"

"OVER TEN TIMES! Janee, you have been suspended over twenty times! What the hell? You're only in the eighth grade," my friend Amari said.

I knew. Shit had gotten pretty crazy after my great-grandpa died while I was in the fourth grade. "I just don't let these hoes run over me. Sometimes it's not even me," I said.

"I feel it," she said. "But are you okay? I know your grandma gets angry a lot. Sometimes she hits you a lot too. My mom and I were just talking about that."

"I'm okay. Don't get me wrong, I do have a smart mouth at times, but it just seems like she will never give me a chance to do anything right; almost as if she's taking her anger out on someone else, and not me. Just yesterday she pulled me by my hair. Girl, and hit me with a skillet because I left a crumb in it when I washed the dishes. She does too much."

"Oh my God. You know my family loves you, and my grandma will definitely take you in if need be!"

"I think I'll stick it out. High school will be a fresh start; maybe I can make her proud."

"That's a good way to look at it! Hey, my b-day is coming up, best friend. We have to develop a plan just like every other holiday, so you can come too! My mama is down."

"How could I forget, you're my best friend. Let me get some paper so we can write this all down."

Later that day.

I was relieved from life as I let out a deep breath, plopped my things onto a chair, and sat on my bed. I immediately began to gaze into the mirror at myself. Earlier, the school called about my arm. No one was there yet, and I was nervous about the outcome.

My anticipation was disturbed by someone busting through my door, "...sitting there cutting because you see that crap on tv. We don't hurt you here; we keep it honest," Uncle Steven said, chastising me.

I gazed. "*Deeper,*" the voices demand, "*deeper as soon as he leaves.*"

Uncle Steven continued, "We had to deal with your crazy ass father, now you! Sheesh, stop stressing me and my mother out. If you continue to open your legs then anyone will continue to take, even your own cousins."

And I did. I enjoyed it and continued because it made me feel beautiful. A princess being rescued by animals, step by step.

I heard myself less and less.

Three days later.

"Janee, they are gone," Ken said. "I don't know when they will be back, so we have to be quick."

"I don't feel like it today," I said, heading for the kitchen.

"What do you mean? You always feel like it. Is it because Josh isn't here this time?" he asked.

"No, I don't feel like it. It doesn't feel right anymore," I said, grabbing a granola bar and then walking back to my room.

"You decide when to just stop? We've been doing this for years. You should've been used to it!" he said.

"You are so weak. You think you can come and make demands whenever you want," I said.

"And you are a bitch. You're lucky I'm talking to you. All you do is steal from Grandma and give the whole family a hard time. Just like your crazy ass father," he said after laughing.

"Let's talk about *your* father. Walking around here like a Disneyland daddy, but not raising y'all. Word on the street is he even has a whole child he doesn't claim," I sneered.

Ken punched me in the arm. "Don't talk about my dad."

"Awe, if only that hurt," I said snarkily, pushing him out my face.

He grabbed my arm and threw me on the bed. "Leave me alone!" I yelled.

"Oh, shut the fuck up! Most of the time you beg for it anyways!" he screamed back.

The next day.

"Hey honey," my older cousin Yasmin said, sitting on my bed, where I lay watching a *Jersey Shore* marathon.

"Hey Yaz," I said, eyes still glued to the tv.

"I'm sorry I had to cancel our girls' day yesterday. I had orders from eBay to ship out," she said.

"It's fine! We can plan another day," I said.

"So, did anything interesting happen yesterday while I was gone?" she asked.

Yaz had been staying with us for the past two months. Turns out, our whole family was looney, and her parents were just as ridiculous as Grandma and Uncle Steven.

"Nope, just watched my shows and stuffed my face," I said.

She paused and looked towards the floor. "Janee, I saw Ken on top of you," she said. I covered my face in my pillow. I was surprised she was just then figured things out. Everyone else had known for years, but swept it under the rug. One time I had heard Uncle Steven say it was good because boys needed the experience.

"Honey, the door was open, and I only came back because I forgot my contacts. I would've stopped it, but I was so loopy because of my meds and all this crap going on with my parents," she explained.

My face remained in the pillow.

"Talk to me, how long had this been going on? Did he rape you?" she asked.

I nodded my head yes. I lied; it had become so much more than that.

"It's okay, I won't tell anyone. I promise," she said. "Now let's go find something to do. I have to get you out of this house."

I'd heard that before.

One week later.

Of course, Yaz didn't keep her promise and told my grandmother about the situation. That was perfect for Grandma! She couldn't stand Ken and finally had a valid excuse to send him back to Arizona. Uncle Steven kept chanting, "You can't rape the willing." I didn't recall at five or six years old asking my eight or nine-year-old cousin to suck his dick or be inside of my ass or pussy. I didn't recall.

But let's fast forward to when I did make myself available. It was because I became comfortable. When I initiated it, it was because I knew I'd be included. I knew they wouldn't be such an ass to me. I knew they would want to stay up and watch movies with me. I did that to feel closer to them. I did that to feel like I belonged. So no, you can't rape the willing, but at that time, I was willing to do anything to have someone on my side, to make me feel important, even if it was only for a moment. And what is willing? Making someone so used to something that even they can't define it? The feeling would come and depart quickly, over and over again. But the only thing that mattered was that the comfort came, not how long it lasted, and that was my truth. What was theirs? No one would touch me unless I said so. I would fight with all I had. I was no longer anyone's sex toy.

Even after Ken moved, I kept getting into trouble. One day, Grandma let me go out with school friends, and I didn't make curfew. As always, I was awarded a three-month punishment, but that time, Uncle Steven had an add on.

"Janee, you need to learn a lesson. You need to learn to be grateful for all that Grandma does for you. We are sending you to your Grandma Cynthia's house for two weeks," he said.

Grandma Cynthia was my father's mother. She was always nice and protected me against Uncle Steven's and Grandmother's verbal and mental attacks. I felt we grew up the same, and somehow, she understood. I was actually quite excited to see her and Grandpa Ray, however, they lived in the projects of Chicago, and I wasn't ready for the roaches either.

We'd finally made it after four hours in the car. Grandma gave me $60 for the two weeks and bought groceries for the house.

Walking into the cluttered apartment, dusty and filled with stuff from the Salvation Army (nothing ever matched, she called it vintage), a roach crawled on the left wall. Seen from my peripheral vision, it showed the worth of the place. *Living Single* played on a decade-old tv that had dust collecting on the antenna, showing the age of the home. Grandma Cynthia sat a plate of spaghetti before my face. Cigarette smoke-stained her skin, her best perfume. There was a bottle on every table in that crowded apartment. Sorry to say they were half empty. I was battling in my head whether this was a safe place to open my mouth or did she already know.

Three days later.

It was time for me and Grandma Cynthia's daily nap. Around 1:30 in the afternoon, she had smoked about seven cigarettes and drank about two and a half bottles of Smirnoff Vodka. It was only natural that she'd have a nap. Grandpa Ray had doubled that by then and relaxed in their bedroom next to the living room. I decided to lay on my back this time, unbuttoning my tight shorts for relief. I dozed off peacefully.

What seemed to be shortly after, I woke up to a hand gently rubbing below my stomach. It felt uncomfortable, and my vagina started to tense up. I looked over quickly and saw a sky-blue button-up shirt, and a black man with jeans on, positioned in a crisscross position beside the couch on the floor. I looked at the face; it was Grandpa Ray. I jumped up quickly, "What are you doing?" I yelled. He got up and walked out the door.

"Grandma! Grandma!" I called as I ran to her room. "Grandma, wake up!" I yelled, shaking her gently. "Grandpa just touched me! Please wake up."

She jumped up, "Where is that mother fucker?" she said, storming out the front door. I followed behind her. She found him at the corner, smoking a cigarette. "Bitch, did you touch my granddaughter?" she yelled.

Throwing his hands up and looking at me, "No, Cynthia, I did not. Janee, how dare you?" he said.

She looked at me.

"Yes, he did, Grandma! I can replay it all to you from my memory," I cried.

"Stay the fuck out of this house," she said to him, grabbing me and walking towards the apartment.

Two hours later, we had ended our conversation with Grandma and Uncle Steven about what occurred, and they made me tell the story over and over again. Uncle Steven threatened to "Fuck Ray up." They said they were on their way to get me, and that they'd be there tomorrow.

Four days later, Uncle Steven and Grandma arrived. They said they had taken their time because I'd made up stories like that before, especially with the whole Ken situation. They said I was lying, but they'd pick me up so that Ray could come home to his wife.

Before getting into the car, Grandma Cynthia pulled me to the side privately. "I did a lot of thinking and wondered why my husband would want your fat ugly ass when he has me. You want me to believe that he would touch you and your saggy titties? You barely know how to wash your ass," she said.

I hopped into the van, crying as always. I told myself no one would touch me without my permission again, and I meant it. No one, no matter what anyone said. No one, not ever again.

When we got home, Yasmin had disappeared, and my punishment continued. My whole summer was gone, and it would shortly be time to go back to school. High school this time! Uncle Steven said every beginning is a new chapter in life. And as a writer, I determined what that chapter would bring. All I could think about writing were the dreams I lived when I was awake. I was torn between being the adult in any and every situation, and just being the blame for it all. All these thought-provoking situations in my life did make me endlessly tired. I decided to take a nap, and I had the oddest dream. It was a dream about a poem, and it was called *Peace At Last.*

I wake up, and it feels awkward and very distant. You don't know how to react; change keeps happening. Memories begin to fade out of sight. You then realize you were never accepted, not in the past, now, not ever. One cannot belong if stability does not exist, and that just may be the true definition of darkness. It's the insane person's place of refuge.

I opened my eyes, and all that made sense rushed to me: I was born to be a disappointment. I was conceived by cruelty and deceit. I was living only to shed, and I would die only to be defeated. I had accepted the insanity once more.

Chapter Four

11 11 P.M. ON 11 11 11

"Janee, have you seen my money?" my grandmother asked after barging into my room.

"Wha-what money, Grandma?" I asked.

"My $300 DTE bill money, did you take it?" she screamed.

First of all, we all knew that money was for the casino tomorrow night. What old person paid their DTE bill in cash? I thought not. Second of all, that may be serious because she was actually looking for it. Usually, I took the money and had my Auntie Ruth cover for me saying that I worked for her and was saving over time. It had worked perfectly the last three times, especially the time coming back from Cedar Point last year.

I would keep lying. "Grandma, why would I take money I don't know about?"

"Check Damon's pocket!" Uncle Steven demanded from down the hall. Pounding on my dad's door, "did you take my mom's money?"

My father rushed out the room. "Nope," he said after pulling out his pockets.

My uncle rolled his eyed and walked away. Sometimes he was such a female! "We will find it Mom!" he yelled out.

I quietly closed my room door. "Why steal from your own grandmother?" people asked and sometimes I even asked myself. Well, it was hard out there. Kind of odd for a fourteen-year-old to say, but it was true.

When I was sick, there was no medication. Once, I had become so ill, my school called my grandmother and told her I could not come back to school until she took me to the doctor. I found out I had strep throat, and after three days, my grandma took away my antibiotics. She was strict about not taking medicine but she never provided any holistic remedies either. By the grace of God, I recovered a week later.

I can even recall the time when I was ten years old, she took me to the gynecologist because she'd had to come up to the school for years whenever I had vaginal pain. She always had some thick white cream to put on it, but it hardly ever worked. Anyway, the doctor examined me, and was horrified at the results. She told me not only did I have BV (Bacterial Vaginosis), but for me to be only ten, my walls were severely damaged. My grandmother made a poor excuse and rushed me out of there immediately.

When I looked up BV, Web MD said it was a buildup of bad bacteria in the vagina that causes an unpleasant odor and discharge. I'd messed up my underwear and smelled since I could remember. It was finally nice to know what I was cursed with. I guessed that all made sense, seeing as I was only allowed to shower and or take a bath once a week. Grandma didn't believe in wasting water but Dad, Uncle Steven, and whoever else that visited was allowed to shower whenever they wanted. Maybe because they contributed to the bills. Birdbaths became my thing, but no matter how many times I washed up, I could not get off all the odor and marks that people had left on me. So, in addition to medicine, I'd buy pads, new underwear, and so on. The only thing I never had to worry about buying was food. See, Grandma and Uncle Steven would let me eat any and everything. True fat asses, we all were. I also found myself buying morning after pills with my Aunt Ruth's parental consent. For those times, I felt my prayers weren't enough to rid me of the capabilities of having a demon child with one of my cousins. My Aunt Ruth always asked why I did what I did with them, but she had never once intervened or convinced me that I should be doing otherwise. I assumed it was okay; everyone knew anyway. There was no way I was confessing my habit of stealing this time. I had finally got the money to pay my new friend Merna's father back for my Erebus ticket, and I was determined to do so.

The next day.

"Merna! Merna!" I called out, hastily walking towards her. "I totally had the money I owe your dad, but I left it at home! Is tomorrow okay?"

"Of course, love. He isn't tripping or anything and neither am I," she said. "Want to come shopping with my mom and I this weekend?"

"That would be great, I will ask my grandma tonight," I said.

I knew repaying my debt would build trust within Merna and our friendship. I left the money hidden deep in my Ugg boots in the back of my closet. It was so obvious, that no one would guess it. Walking up to my driveway after getting off the bus, Uncle Steven met me at the garage door. "Hey Tio," I said.

"Hey honey, we have to talk," he said.

"About what?" I asked.

"Did you steal Grandma's money?" he asked. I stared blankly at him.

"Janee, Grandma had cameras put up in the house. If you took the money, she will be able to see it. She is checking them tonight. If you took the money, you need to tell me now, so I can cover for you and return the money," he said.

"I did! Please help me Uncle Steven. I needed things, and I needed to pay my friend back for Erebus," I said.

"I got your back, honey. Just don't do it again," he said.

I quickly went into the house after nodding my head. I didn't see Grandma anywhere. I headed straight to my room.

Two hours later.

There was a knock at my door, and Uncle Steven opened it, "Janee, Grandma wants to speak to you," he said.

I got up quickly and walked towards the family room. I saw Grandma sitting on the sofa, carefully making jewelry and an open spot next to her. Uncle Steven had his beads and wire out making jewelry as well. They both were probably more so listening to *Jeopardy* as I noticed it playing on the screen.

"You stole my money," my grandmother said.

I glanced at my uncle.

"Don't look at me!" he demanded.

My grandma looked up at me. My whole body shook like an unexpected sugar rush.

"Yes," I whispered.

She hastily jumped up and grabbed me by my hair, and started screaming at me. Quicker than a glimpse, she started punching me in my face, and I began hitting her in the head. My uncle jumped up, "Don't touch my mother," and knocked me down. He got on top of me, punching me in my face. Suddenly, he stopped and looked back; it was my dad watching him.

"Call the police, Janee," my dad said as he ran away from my uncle.

My uncle grasped the black metal poker from the fireplace and chased my father down the hallway. My grandma followed screaming, "No!" as my uncle challenged, her voice repeating, "I am going to kill him. I've had enough."

Ten minutes later.

"Janee, let me see," my grandmother said, reaching to wipe off my bloody face in the bathroom. She was trying to calm me down because the police were right outside the door.

After nearly fifteen minutes arguing with my family about what had occurred and who was to blame, I was taken to safety by a female police officer named Sarah. I told her I had someone to call and stay with for the night. That person was my brother, Jerrod, and Aunt Ruth. In approximately twenty minutes, they both came and took me straight home.

"I am running you a bath, Janee," my aunt said. "It was wrong of you to take your grandma's money. I can only cover for you so much."

"Yeah, you could've just asked us for help," my brother said.

"Always, and you can't go around hitting people's mother," my aunt said.

"I know, Auntie, but she hits me all the time. Yaz, said one day I'll get tired of her hitting me. Whether I deserved it this time or not, I was tired of her always hitting me," I said.

"We understand, but there are other ways," my brother said. "All that is done is done, you are here now, and you are safe."

"You can call your cousin, Yaz, to tell her what happened after your bath," My aunt said. "I know she's eager to hear from you."

"Love you guys," I said.

"We love you too," they said in unison.

They both left me alone with my thoughts. It was November 11, 2011. At that point, I had a heart that was born to be broken, a mind meant for corruption, and a soul traveling with no destination. I was a person built due for destruction.

There was a knock at the door interrupting my thoughts, "Janee, its Mom's birthday," my brother said as he left the bathroom, leaving a pink towel on the counter, before closing the door behind him. Some people's births are like deaths. Happy birthday Mo

Chapter Five

TOO, TWO FACED

This isn't a long chapter, very straightforward, with no questions left to answer, in my own words. Six months later, I found myself in my room, crowded by isolation. It was starting again: yeah, that urge to cut. Why wasn't anything I did good enough? Yaz was mad about me cleaning up again. I just didn't get it. I was upholding a 3.5 GPA, and I had gotten up every day, nothing past 9 a.m., to clean the house. I made one complaint about Makya not cleaning up, and got shunned for 48 hours.

Makya was my play cousin. When I was living with my aunt as a toddler, she was there before both my brother and me. She had the education of a seventh grader for some odd reason, even though we were both fourteen. Auntie said she wasn't able to get back into school, and she had a baby. Thank God she let that one live. She must have been in love with the dad. Makya and I used to play too. She taught me a few things that helped me satisfy girls better. We stopped when I moved back in, however. We'd actually become quite close; we watched the *Bad Girls Club* together, and *Love and Hip Hop*. We loved eating enchiladas, nachos, and talking shit. We hardly ever argued; it was great. Auntie tried to turn us against each other. She would put little bugs in our ears about one another individually, and Jerrod was quite distant then. It was like he was disappointed in me or something. We barely spoke, and he brought up my name a lot to Auntie. They loved talking shit. I did what I was supposed to do; what could they have to say?

"Come eat!" Auntie said after bursting through my door. She, of course, slammed the door like she did every night. It was even worse on Sundays after she got home from church.

I slowly got out of bed, still bummed over the fact that Yaz wouldn't talk to me.

Makya was already in the kitchen. We giggled when we saw each other, grabbed our plates, and headed downstairs. She slept on the couch downstairs. Auntie said she was going to fix her up another room in the basement, but she still hadn't cleared out all her and Jerrod's storage. Jerrod's room was in the basement as well. And no, there wasn't any funny business going on with them! I was pretty sure he was gay. About two months ago, Makya and I were snooping on his laptop, and in his history was gay porn, hardcore gay porn. I'd wished he'd just come out. In a heated argument, Makya brought it up, and he just froze. Oops!

Two months later.

I heard a knock at my bedroom door. I got up after quickly pulling my earbuds out my ear. It clearly wasn't Auntie because there wasn't an outburst. I opened the door, and there stood my brother.

"Janee, I found mom!" he exclaimed.

"Wha-what! How? Where? When?!" I screamed.

"Just now, on Facebook, look," he said, leading me to the computer room.

I looked fixedly at the screen; I saw this burnt caramel toned woman with flashy jewelry and blue eyeshadow. I judged that her whole life clashed by the looks of her profile. As much as I wanted to be happy, he found her, questions clouded my mind, and rage built inside my heart.

"Janee, I can't believe it's her," Jerrod said in amazement.

"I just want to know how, after all these years of knowing that she has two teenage children, she didn't think to even check social media to find us?" I asked.

"Janee, please don't start. Her page seems fairly new. Don't jump to conclusions," he said.

"How can I not! She left us, and no one can make me believe that she has been on this devoted search for us, it'd be a lie!" I fussed.

"We don't know the whole stor..."

"What is going on in here?!" Auntie said, marching into the room.

"Look, Auntie, it's mom," Jerrod jumped up.

Auntie gazed at the screen, "Well look at that! Do you feel relieved?" she asked him, like she really cared. The attention had swayed from her to mom instantly. He nodded his head. "Don't worry about what Janee has to say! If she wants to be negative, then leave her be," she said, walking out.

I rolled my eyes as I watched her leave the room. "Well, what now?" I asked my brother.

"I've reached out on OUR behalf," he said.

"Sounds good," I said, teasingly and closed the door behind myself.

That was going to cause some shit, some mighty smelly shit at that.

Later that night.

Jerrod sat beside me on the basement couch as I flipped from channel to channel. Makya had left for the weekend to visit her mom. It would be interesting when she returned because every time she left and came back, there was an issue. Auntie always fussed about her attitude, but it was none of my business.

"Mom responded," he said.

"Oh yeah. What'd she say?" I asked.

"Well, Auntie said she could move up here and stay with us until she gets on her feet." I sat up straight and looked him in his eyes. "So, she'll be here Monday night."

"Wooowww, just like that?" I whined.

"Please be hopeful like you used to be when we were younger," he pushed.

Jerrod always had a good heart. Even when we were just kids, he'd protect me and anyone else in his presence. He was a saint in every adults' opinion that crossed his path. He was a true angel; I just didn't understand why he always chose to be distant from me since I moved in, as though I was on his turf or something.

Monday night.

The night had come; Auntie, Jerrod, and I pulled up to the greyhound bus station, and there sat a woman on a bench. She had on a brown scarf, covering her forehead, with curly black hair coming out of the sides. She wore dark, washed blue jeans and a striped black and grey shirt, with a red cami peeking out the top. "Mom," (I should have said "mother" because I was still pissed). We embraced, and auntie bought us each a chicken dinner. It wasn't long, and there wasn't much conversation to decide that she would stay at our house and live there for good. She was home, and I was okay with that.

Weeks passed by, and our relationship strengthened. As it did, she and Jerrod's became skeptical. She noticed the way Auntie and Jerrod treated me, and we began having secrets. Auntie was sweet as pie in front of mom and even went as far as to put a bug in her ear of how jealous I was of Jerrod.

There was a time I was Jerrod's biggest fan; yeah, that's my brother. We'd do talent shows at home, and I'd sit and listen to him write songs. I remember when he found out I could sing; he was so proud. While I was living at Grandmother's, I'd leave him voicemails of me singing whenever he didn't answer. Yaz butted in from time to time, claiming how clingy and manipulative I was. I wondered if she was just jealous that I rarely wept much over her.

My mother's forever was short-lived; she disappeared right after Christmas and left me to fight alone. I can't explain how many apologies I had to say that I never meant. I was not that crazy.

Auntie kept an attitude, and I became increasingly defiant. I stole just to steal and lied because I knew it would piss her off. She, of course, ran to Yaz, and Yaz always threatened to kick my ass and would ignore me for days. Yaz had a soft spot for Auntie and had adopted her as family. Neither one of them saw me.

Yasmin

"I can assure you, no man wants a fat ass girlfriend. I told you about my guy friend that had a big girl. She was such a good woman to him, but he would not claim her because she was big. I have some friends with sons, but they wouldn't look your way because of your weight. Get it together, and I got you." Yasmin was something interesting, somewhat my biggest enemy but my favorite person. She was there when I needed her at Grandmother's, and I enjoyed talking to her. I barely saw her, but she was herself, and I loved her. She wished to raise confidence in me academically and physically, but she claimed that it could only be done through losing weight. I was slim when my mom was around; the attention from guys overwhelmed me, and besides, it's hard to paint a picture when you don't like what you see.

Auntie Ruth

I'd clean, I'd compliment, I aimed to improve my grades, and tried to stay out the way, but nothing did the trick. She said I did everything for attention, but it became the thing to do, to try to master death. Did she want me here? I knew she loved me, but what had changed? She should've felt safe knowing that I didn't need her. She had two faces, but I was the "crazy" one.

Part 2: Superficial

There I sat in my therapist Claire's room reading my wellness plan. I was allowed to read what Auntie had to say. Only one word stood out, and that was "superficial." Clair wrote, "One day, Janee sat in the bathroom and cut herself using a razor blade she broke off her shavers. She cut her left arm until there were superficial cuts up and down her arm. I can assume she wanted attention. In her court files, there was questionable abuse by her grandfather (her mother's father) and by other family members. She seems to act out for attention. I can't get through to her."

Superficial, that's all I read. Superficial. I laid looking at my arm wrapped in gauze. The doctor said it was almost deep enough to need stitches. They didn't keep me on suicide watch because I lied. I always lied. I lied in middle school when the teachers became suspicious and called home. I lied and said I cut because the kids kept calling me a big 'ole monkey. Last week when I did cut, Yaz refused to come see me. She said that's what I would want her to do. For her to go out of her way and enable me. Who cared if I ached for attention? I was willing to risk it all for someone to care, for anyone to be proud of me. Cries of the insane, does anyone hear me?

Grandma Susan

I had known Grandma Sue since I'd known anything. Jerrod is my half-brother, and with that being said, Grandma Sue was his grandmother. She comforted me with tears in her eyes and said, as she rewrapped my arm, "You are more precious and worth far more than all the gold in the world." As she saw my grades improve, she volunteered to take me and pick me up from school. We'd go shopping all on her, dollar show movie dates, and trips to Target. Von Muar was her spot, and in return, she bought me the best shoes and clothes. After every outing, she'd say, "Alright, I'm done with you taking all my money." I knew she was joking because with every good grade came another outing, and I kept the grades coming. Although she was a grandma, she knew how to dress, and she taught me how to do so. Every time I came home, I was greeted at the door by Auntie, "Sue is Jerrod's grandma, don't forget that." I was never glad to be home.

Jerrod

"That fake shit isn't cutting it! For all I care, you can go out in the middle of the street and play in traffic," I said, pointing at Jerrod.

"YOU'RE ACTING ALL TOUGH, BUT YOU'RE NOT GOING TO DO ANYTHING," Jerrod yelled.

"YOU LIKE TO PUSH PEOPLE. IN A MINUTE I WON'T HAVE ANY CONTROL. I CANNOT STAND YOU! I HATE YOU SO MUCH," I screamed.

Why say this to my brother? Well, when you have someone preaching one thing in your ear and then whispering the total opposite in another person's ear, it drives you mad. Blood is thicker than water? Yeah right. First off, that isn't even the whole quote, and what people don't understand is the word 'family' or 'relatives' doesn't mean shit to me. I create my own family which, means I'll cut off anyone by any means necessary. What kind of blood questions rape, what kind of blood backstabs you, and does it so effortlessly? Not any kin of mine.

One week later.

"Jerrod has all this shit, Janee. He doesn't do shit but act all goody two shoes and gets whatever he wants. Auntie swears he's an angel," Makya said, observing Jerrod's clothes and shoes. "Like who the fuck does he think he is with all these suits?"

"I am screaming! This nigga has everything. He pisses me off. Auntie is always fussing about me being jealous of him, well I'd love to do some jealous shit," I said

"Like what? Burn his shit?" Makya said after a chuckle.

"No, I don't want his shit to disappear. I want him to see all his shit destroyed," I said, picking up a bottle of bleach.

"Awwww shit. Let's do it!" Makya said.

After bleaching ALL of Jarrod's shoes and clothes, Makya and I decided to watch our favorite show, *Bad Girls Club*, how befitting. Sitting there, I didn't feel bad about what I'd decided to do. My heart was broken; I had no clue what tore Jerrod and me up. We used to be inseparable, and he'd protect me and lift me up. Now we'd walked past each other like we both didn't exist. I thought I was doing better. I thought things would change. I was only making things worse. No one chooses or accepts my efforts. Surface level pain? Surface level insanity? Or maybe it was deeper than what anyone concluded.

One month later, Auntie put in a request for me to be moved out of her home. She assured me that it was because Jerrod was sleeping in the basement and hat the social worker deemed that unfit. She lied, and she gave up. Should've never pushed me to my limits, good riddance.

The Seventh Thought: On My Mama

I was listening to a YouTube video by Apostle Gabriel M. McCullum, and this statement spoke to me,

"God deals with us in stages of development. Nothing happens without order; God does nothing without order. God is using those uncomfortable moments to establish Himself- to get your attention. Your bad news and unpleasant moments are an opportunity for God to establish who you will become. You can't understand experience with no conflict. Experience is the best teacher! God wants to make you great."

Things had been shaking for me lately, and I was vexed. I was confused, and I was uncomfortable. My heart and spirit were unsettled because of "everyone's" most important and favorite earthy person- their mother.

A mother is, supposedly, a girl's best friend; I struggled with believing this. Why do people become easily offended when their mother is criticized? Why were my peers in foster care still heavily connected to their mothers? Why isn't the love lost? She isn't there, correct? They're in foster care, right? She abused them, yes? I didn't understand. The only person on this earth that was supposed to be there for me, my biggest fan, and my number one nurse- wasn't there. And that narrative was bound to break me.

I remember how beautiful she was the day I met her again in the summer of 2015. Although she was dressed simply in a scarf, striped fitted T-shirt, and dark washed jeans, she was stunning. I remember growing up, and hoping to look like her to give me a reason to love myself and fully believe it, because I thought she was beautiful.

I can't count how many times I'd write my mother a letter or was eager to spend time with my grandparents Luke and Carol, just to hear about her. I remember spending time with Jerrod and just basking in the few memories he had with her. Dad told me stories about her. How he wasn't the only one, and how she was a get around girl. I heard many stories about why and how she left, that she didn't want her kids and left them for drugs. She came back up north to fight for us, not to live with Luke and Carol, and again, I heard how she was a get around girl.

I heard them saying she was in a group home (Children's Village to be exact) because of her lies. I knew about being locked up. And when a cage seems better than "home," something is up. God, I wish I knew what a good happy ending feels like, I still think they are make-believe. Even when she came back once more, I fell in love with her again. But, she'd take the things that I'd worked for and apologize with hand-me-downs. If there were earrings on my dresser, that was an "I'm sorry." If my Juicy Couture purses were missing, maybe it was because I did something wrong.

Ephesians 6:1-4, "Children, obey your parents in the Lord, for this is right. Honor your father and mother, which is the first commandment with promise; so that it may go well with you and that you may live long in the land." Why? And how could I honor someone that was never there or that chose to leave repeatedly?

"Don't you ever speak on my Mama! On my Mama, bro, I will slap you!" Don't mind me; I'm practicing the embitterment that'll one day rise when someone speaks ill of my mother, which is if someone remembers I even have one. Happy Mother's Day to the Mom that out beat the rest, the mom that has always been there for me even when I did not want her to be. The mom that I call my rock, number one fan, headache, and heartbeat. I love you forever. I still feel nothing.

Hmmm, what are the qualities of a mother? I don't know myself. In fact, I had to ask others and use Google. Here is what I came up with:

- Loving (unconditionally)
- Balanced
- Wise
- Compassionate
- Willing to teach
- Willing to give time
- Patient
- Survivor
- Strong
- Empathetic

All these qualities are good. They correlate with health and love- with happiness. I was not well. I did not feel loved and I lacked happiness. Where was she? Where was MY mother?

There is a version of me from you. We share the same pain, and as a part of my purpose and lifestyle for change, I ask, how do we fault someone that doesn't know? That does not know from right and wrong or how to even properly survive.. My whole point of being a future woman in power is to thoroughly access each person that comes before me. To give them the opportunity to tell their story and victimization, how they survived and finally touch the root of it all, "Why did they do it?" So, I don't forgive you. I can't. But with all my soul, all the right in me, all my pure qualities that the Lord has gifted me, I want to.

My ever-longing need for God, and His grace is what brings the good of my heart. It fills my heart to know that I have someone forever that will accept and forgive my truths. It helps me escape from seriousness and the need to be perfect even in pain and lack because that is impossible. Thus, I will forgive you because I want to. My heart is begging me to. And truthfully, you deserve all the forgiveness to even be alive after the cage they trapped you in. But what made it worse is the fact that they carefully decorated it. The detailing of the beauty on that hell they enslaved you in was inconceivable. I don't forgive you at this moment, but I want to.

God, please grant mercy on me as I tussle with the forgiveness and love for my mother. You know our stories and who we will be. I am asking for a healthy future for us and love for one another to follow. Lord, please forgive us for choosing what we thought was better for ourselves and our loved ones instead of consulting You first. Thank You for pulling us out of situations and keeping us. Thank You for the sound mind and heart to change You have gifted unto me. Lord, thank You, thank You, thank You for using us both as vessels. We love You. Amen.

Chapter Six

FOR THE LOVE OF ENGLISH

A tan door opened with Ms. Demarco beside it, after I knocked on it twice. "Hello, Janee. Have a seat, sweetie," she said with a welcoming smile.

As I walked into her office, memories of being in her presence rushed into my mind. I've always loved and admired Vice Principal Demarco. She had been by my side since the ninth grade. And trust me, I had inflicted several headaches on her. I'd been doing great this year- awards for grades, special achievements. It was a shocking and also quick turnaround. So, I could only imagine what she'd called me down for.

"Janee," she said, "Tell me about your relationship with Mr. Paolini."

I felt my heart drop. Gulp. I swallowed before answering. "I mean, we have had our ups and downs. But we have worked through them to make the classroom environment better for both of us," I said, trying to hide the fear hidden behind my words.

Ms. Demarco began studying me with her brown eyes. One soft hand rested beneath her chin, the fingers of the other tapped lightly on her desk.

"With your help, of course," I added with a huge nervous smile. Oh, my gaaawwd! What does she know!? I thought.

She pulled her computer monitor towards me and, with a raised eyebrow, asked, "So, what is this email?"

Fuck. "Wh-what email?" I questioned, looking around stupidly. "Is it pertaining to that Lord of the Flies essay due next week?"

She shook her head. "You know the exact email this is pertaining to Miss Dukes."

I stared blankly.

"You can start talking now, including the truth, or stay silent, or lie and suffer the consequences later."

Tears started rolling down my cheeks while my leg shook quicker every second.

Handing me a tissue, she continued. "Mr. Paolini brought this email you sent him to my attention Tuesday after school." I was still silent; my eyes lowered. She paused. "Maybe I can refresh your memory." She put on her reading glasses. "It reads on April 18, 2013, at 7:56 p.m.:

Rani,

I can't believe summer is almost here! I'm going to miss you, and that's why I need your number. You make me mad, but you're so cute, and I love those arms, and that big....you know.

Write back,
Janee

"Have I refreshed your memory, dear?" she smirked.

"Yes," I replied with my eyes sealed to the floor. "It's all my fault," I began, "I was just so excited to have another person care about me. It was hard for me to leave him alone," I attempted to defend him.

I'd rather take all the blame. People always had things to say. Someone probably snitched. I didn't want him to lose his job. He had a whole degree, and I was only 17, I could afford to take the fall.

"Are you sure you're not leaving things out? I'm going to ask you again. Will you please describe your relationship with your English teacher, Mr. Paolini?" I stared in confusion. She continued, "I have had several reports of you taking up his time and being disruptive in his class." I blinked. "Reports have confirmed that you have taken several pictures of him in class, made several inappropriate comments to him in class, and so on. I need the full story, sweetie, and I need it now."

"Yes, ma'am," I replied, rolling my eyes slightly. "It all began my sophomore year when I first met him, I was...."

The bell rang.

"Where is this broad?" I asked in disgust. "The first time I do my homework, trying to better myself this trimester, and she decides not to show up. It's the first day of the second trimester!"

Chase, one of my goofy classmates, turns to me. "Janee, you didn't hear?" I looked at him in confusion. "Mrs. Dravidian won't be here for the rest of the year!"

With a smile on my face, "Whaaaa, I'm paralyzed with happiness. Do you know what this means, Chase?!"

"Yesssss! We can eat in class now!"

With my mouth pulled to the side, I grimed at his foolishness for three seconds. "No child, it means an easy A."

"Oh yeah. That too."

Turning away from him, I saw one of my close classmates, Clarissa. I waved my hands to catch her attention, so she'd sit with me.

Before sitting, she looked at me with a smirk, "Now, Janee, you know Mrs. Dravidian has assigned seats, and she will flip out on us."

"The absent can't flip out on the present," I said with a big smile. "She's gone for the year!" I screeched.

"Yaaaaaaas," we said in unison.

We both glanced up and saw Misty standing in front of us, preparing to sit down.

Who would've ever thought that after bullying her all freshman year, Misty would become one of my very best friends?

"I heard y'all. You got the snacks 'Nae?" she asked with her hand reached out, and Clarissa grinned.

Smiling, I dug into my bookbag and said, "Duh, three watermelon Arizona's and three packs of watermelon sour patch kids. I'm most definitely the plug."

"Ooooouuu," they said, with a huge smile.

"So, now that we have the snacks, I have a story for y'all." Clarissa and Misty's eyes bulged out in interest. "When I went to the mall Saturday, I met..."

"Hey guys! Can I please have your attention?"

As the class looked toward the front of the room we saw...well, I saw this beautiful man. He had black slacks on with a black dress shirt. His skin was beautifully pale, hair short but no buzzing and his medium-sized nose gave everything about his roots away.

"Thank you! I am Mr. Paolini, and I will be your long-term substitute teacher."

Now he was definitely worthy of an 'ooooouu.'

After hearing his last name, my ideas about his roots were confirmed, and instantly I raised my hand the highest it could be raised, "Are you Italian?" He smiled. "Because you look just like Vinny from Jersey Shore," I continued. The class laughed, and whispers of agreement began to flood the room. He blushed.

Chase provoked the foolishness, "GET CRAZY, GET LOUD!"

The class chimed in, "LETS PARTY! GET LOUD," in unison, "IF YOU WANNA HAVE FUN THEN DO SOMETHING. IF YOU WANNA HAVE FUN THEN DO SOMETHING CRAAAAAAZYYYY." Rani laughed hysterically.

After our performance, I continued, "So, you're Italian, right?"

"Haha, that's correct. I come from a typical Italian family. My parents were born in Italy, and how my mother cooks reminds me of it all the time."

I gasped.

Misty, chimed in, "Mr. P.," she paused. "Is it okay if I call you that?" He nodded, and smiled "How old are you?" Misty asked. The room gasped collectively. She continued, "Because you look really young."

"What an odd question," he said after a laugh. "But um...I turned 30 in October."

"Ain't God good," I accidentally said out loud.

Mr. P. looked at me and smiled as the class laughed hysterically.

The bell rang.

Breaking up the laughter, "Haha, okay, class, we will all get more acquainted tomorrow." I smiled at him. "See you all then."

We waved and said our goodbyes in unison as well as one by one.

The next day.

"Heyyyy yaalll," Mr. P. joked as he waved his hand hello. This was his first of many attempts at being a 'hood rat'.

"Heyyyy," the class said in unison.

"The first thing we are going to get into this trimester is The Great Gatsby by. F. Scott Fitzgerald."

"But wait-," my classmate Victor interrupted, "You said we could get more acquainted today, Mr. P.," he continued.

"Right! Well, first things first. I absolutely despise the ratchets," he answered.

The class burst out laughing.

"Haha. rat-like behavior will not be tolerated on my watch," he continued. "When I was in high school, I wore all black and was considered an outcast. That didn't bother me because I didn't care for people anyways," he joked.

"Where are the pictures?" I asked.

"Yeah! Let's see 'em, P.," Chase agreed.

"Depending on how you guys do on the book essay, showing off my pictures can be determined," he teased.

"AN ESSAY!" the class yelled in confusion.

"Yaaaaasssss," I said with excitement. The class grimed me, but Mr. P. smiled. "I lovvveee a good essay."

The bell rang.

A month later.

"What did you get on Mr. P.'s essay?" I asked after waving Misty down in the hallway.

"A freaking C-, bitch," she whined. "What did you get?"

"An A+," I blushed.

Rolling her eyes, she responded, "Of course you did." I looked at her, confused. "Mr. Paolini adores you. You're like a teacher's pet, but it's so much different with him. He brags about your work all the time." she continued.

"Don't make me blush," I said.

"You already did," she mocked.

"But girl, he loves all his students, and everyone loves him." Misty rolled her eyes. I continued, "I don't see the difference."

Coming down the stairs, Kiesha butted in, "Ohhhh my Goooddd! How could you not!" I looked at her with my neck thrown back in shock. "Every time we see him it's, 'Janee, you are so smart' or if you're not around, 'Guys, where's Janee? Is she okay?'" she said, mimicking his voice.

"Byeeeeeeee. PAHAHHAHAHA! You sound just like that nigga," I said. "I'm so glad you transferred into our class." Kiesha smiled.

"Just like him. That's crazy," Misty said. "But it's true." Kiesha nodded her head in agreement. "It's almost as if he's in love with you."

"Who? Mr. Peanut butter man?" I yelped.

"Bitch, you did NOT just call him that," Kiesha said.

"I like it," Misty said.

Shit, and I was in love with him too. And who is that? MR. PEANUT BUTTER MAN.

I know this sounds cliché and whatnot, or even like a Sunday night Lifetime movie, you know that whole "teacher-student relationship" crap. But don't bug out your eyes too much! I wasn't that crazy.

"Guys, have you all finished your daily prompt on the board?" Mr. Paolini asked, trying to take charge.

"Don't worry, Mr. P! We got you," Sean, another classmate, winked.

"Gee, thanks, Sean. I couldn't handle this class without you," Mr. P joked sarcastically.

"Yes, Yaz...no, no, no, he doesn't care that I'm talking on the phone... Yaz, because I'm his favorite, of course." The class stared at me. Yaz had finally answered her phone for me a few days back. "Yes, I saw the picture. Yaaaaassss girl, yaaaaas-"

"Janee!" Mr. P summoned.

"One second, Yaz. Yes?" I asked.

"Remove your cellular device from your ear instantly."

"But wait," I pleaded. "My cousin wants to talk to you," I said, and handed him the phone.

"Hello, yes, yes it is..."

Oy. I wondered what she was saying. She owed me big.

"Yes, Janee is one of my best students... (he listened) she behaves most of the time," he said, chuckling. I raised my left eyebrow in confusion. "Haha, no. She's really great. She has the highest grade in my class."

Now, why in the hell was he talking about me? They were supposed to be getting acquainted. They were the Match, and I was the dot com!

"Ay," Misty said, tapping my shoulder. Kiesha looked at me in confusion. "Why are you giving away your man?" I smacked my lips. "Girl, please. Y'all got something going on." Kiesha nodded with a cheesy smirk.

Mr. P. listened again on the phone. "Nice talking to you too. Take care." He hung up and handed me back my phone.

I stared at him with my eyes enlarged, hoping to go to a wedding in a few months.

"She said to call her whenever you get ratchet."

The class burst with laughter.

Well gah damn. Ain't no cake then, huh? So much for matchmaker. I'm taking my dot com and moving along. Ain't this bout a bit-

"Can't try to give away what belongs to you," Misty teased as Kiesha winked at me.

Rolling my eyes and shushing them away, "Mr. Paolini?"

"Yes, Janee? I know your prompt is done and accurate. So, what's up?" He answered with a smile.

I smiled. "Are you single?"

"I'M TOO DEAD!" Chase interrupted. The class looked from him to me back and forth. "I'm so dead that I'm not even alive anymore," Chase said through a laugh.

The bell rang.

He glanced at me, then turned his attention back to the class, "If you don't have that prompt done, have it tomorrow. I'm serious, you guys," Mr. P. said as the class walked out the room. "Janee," he whispered. I stopped and looked at him before reaching the door. He motioned me to come closer and whispered, "I am single," then he smiled.

Yaaaaaas, I said to myself as I walked out. Is that Daddy or naw?

When I returned home, I decided to call Yaz. "Hi child," she said, answering my call.

"Yasmin! I got an A on my social studies quiz," I said in excitement.

"Good. Next time let's aim for an A+," she said. "What's that, Keith? Keith is being nosey, hold on. Yes, the child got another A. Keith says good job."

"Thanks, Baba," I said with a huge smile.

"I'm proud of you for doing what you're supposed to be doing."

Sophomore year had been such a turnaround for me. Who would've thought the girl who had a 1.6 GPA Freshman year, got two Fs and three

D-s first semester, would be pulling all As and Bs? That was just the beginning! I couldn't wait to see what next year would bring.

"Nae," Misty said, walking up to me.

"Hey," I answered as I continued walking down the hallway.

"How's everything going with your mom? Are you happy she's back after she left again and all? And I know you're getting ready to leave your aunts too," she said.

Uneasy, I replied, "It's going well. My aunt is still acting weird. My brother…he, and I are trying to bond despite the bleach incident. But I don't know. I just-"

"Is everything okay, Janee?" Mr. P. asked. "I noticed you weren't in class today. Are you okay?"

Looking around the hallway, then back at the ground, I replied, "I'm okay, I guess. Just a lot going on."

The warning bell rang.

Stepping away, "Well, I have to get to class," Misty said. Looking at Mr. P with a smile, "I trust you'll take good care of her." He smiled as she turned and walked away.

Turning his attention back at me, "Can you stay for a little while after school?" I nodded my head. "Great, see you then."

As he walked away, I had to stop and think. I wasn't sure what it was or where it was going, but I did know that I had found not only another supporter but someone who looked beyond what everyone else saw. All the unruly parts enticed him, the good traits lingered on his mind.

A few months later.

Quickly sitting at the lunch table, I had to blurt something out and super-fast. "Yallllllll."

Looking around frantically, Kiesha and Misty answered in unison, "What?!"

"Can you guys please stay after school with me?"

"All the times you've stayed after school with Rani (that's right, we were on first name bases), you're still nervous?" Misty teased.

Butting in, "Yeah, haha. Y'all must really be in love." I grinned. "Still in the cupcake phase, huh?" she teased.

Rolling my eyes, "Look hoes, is it a yes or a no?"

"Duh!" they yelled.

"So, what's the excuse this time, 'cause you're definitely not in any of his classes anymore?" Misty asked.

"Editing an essay, duh. You know this."

Misty and Kiesha smirked in regards to the obvious.

After school.

I sat in one of the desks at the front of the room. Rani and I took turns repeatedly glancing at one another as he spun in his chair at the desk until I mustered up the courage to break the silence. "How was your childhood? You never talk about it. Every time someone asks you skate around the question." He stared at me for a few seconds then looked straight down at the ground.

Misty and Kiesha should've never left us alone.

"Well, um," he cleared his throat. "You already know I was very gothic. Everyone thought I was emo in school. I didn't really have many friends. I just kind of existed. At home too, really. My older brother harassed me, haha. Kicking my ass and doing rude things like trying to stuff me into a suitcase. I just never felt like I belonged anywhere. Which is why I dislike people and stay to myself," he answered, still looking at the ground.

Looking up to the ceiling, I responded, "I figured that." He quickly looked up.

"How so?"

"I read people well."

"Ahhh!" he said, and his face lit up. "I knew when I told you to listen to that song I Read You Like an Open Book by Tages that you would realize it's related to you. The shoe fits." I smiled. "So, what meds do you take?" he asked.

Stunned, I quickly looked at him and then began shaking my head, "Zoloft," I said, trying not to sound too embarrassed.

"So, you're right on the borderline of being bipolar." My eyes remained glued to the floor. "I had a girlfriend that took Zoloft too."

Rolling my eyes, "And how long did that last?" I responded sarcastically.

"Haha," he smiled, looking at me. "Not very long- short actually," he pushed out through giggles.

With my face lit up, "So, does that make me crazy?"

He looked at me for a minute without responding and said, "No, it means you're real- I'm happy to know you exist."

Staying after school with him became a daily thing. It kept my grades up, and I had someone else to be honest with. I told him everything that I could ever tell a person and everything that I couldn't. We could communicate with absolutely no sounds or hints. I guess you could call this cliché shit. The year was almost up, and one conversation had to take place and definitely with words.

"El oh el. Why do you keep staring at me?" Rani asked through constant blushes.

I smiled and looked away and then back at him, "You know why," I finally said.

"Ughhh, you know what the answer is."

"I'm not sure because it hasn't been clear, and you know I have a weird way of making you change your mind," I said with a grin.

He laughed, "The summer..."

Butting in, "And summertime sadness it will be for me if-"

"I told you after graduation," he interrupted.

We smiled at each other for a few minutes.

Getting out of my seat, I approached him. "Can I at least get a hug?" I asked with a huge smile and opened my arms.

"Always," he said, embracing me, just as he accidentally grazed my right boob.

Kiesha and Misty charged through the door, startling us. "Oooooop; ooooouuu," they said in unison. We quickly broke away from each other, and I began gathering my things.

"Hey guys," Rani said, trying to act normal.

"Oop. Hey, Mr. P.," they said. Why do these hoes always speak in harmony? I thought.

Grabbing their arms, "Let's go, girls," I said, and rushed them out the door.

"Bye, Janee," Rani said.

I waved.

With no inch of a whisper, "That's definitely your nigga," Kiesha said while Misty nodded her head.

That was one of the last times I spoke to Rani Paolini...BEFORE THE SUMMER OF COURSE! This is a two-year story, y'all. The summer was filled with the very least of awesomeness. It was the summertime sadness I had predicted, and I missed Rani dearly. The conversations with Kiesha and Misty weren't enough to ease my frustration. And unfortunately, we weren't able to hang out as much. Junior year was going to be different. More friend time, less headache. Nothing was going to hold me back, and I was one year closer to being grown, and by being grown, I mean being grown with Rani Paolini. Last year's grades were on point, I had my same friends, and new weave—let's go!

The bell rang.

The hallways were filled with kids of all levels dispersing to their classrooms.

Kiesha nudged me as she snuck a whisper, "You excited, bitch?" she asked.

"Whattt are youuu talking abouttt?" I yelled- my voice carried.

"Miss Dukes and Miss Davis! Quiet, we are listening to the alto's part in Gloria," Mrs. London, our choir teacher, yelled from the piano.

We smiled.

Kiesha continued in a whisper, "You know," she smiled sheepishly. "Have you seen Rani, yet?"

I rolled my eyes while smiling, "Girrrrrll-"

"I'm not going to tell you again, ladies. Please stop talking," Mrs. London scorned.

Middle Eastern Night.

"Hey, chica," my Spanish teacher, Mrs. Rayas, said.

"Hey, Azal!" I replied.

"Hey," she chastised, "what did I tell you about calling me by my first name?" She smiled.

"Lo siento, Señora," I said with a smile.

"Are you still helping us out with the Middle Eastern Culture Night after school today?"

"Of course, wallah" I confirmed, using the Arabic word for 'I swear to God'.

Later after school.

As I turned into another hallway of the school with a box of henna in my arms, I looked up and saw Rani walking toward me, smiling. I smiled back and continued walking toward him. He held both his hands out, trying to show off his white thobe with gold lining.

"What do you think?" he asked, looking at himself up and down.

I burst out laughing, "You're beautiful-Jamila- that's Arabic for 'beautiful'."

"Shukraan," he thanked me in Arabic.

"Ahhh, Chica," Mrs. Rayas gasped in excitement. "You brought the henna."

As Mrs. Rayas and I were talking, I could see Rani staring at me through the corner of my eyes. He had a bad habit of doing that. People often questioned me, asking if we had something going on. I'd always laugh it off, hoping they were joking. As the feelings grew deeper, I guess people's eyes widened.

"Wow, Mr. Paolini, you are looking very angelic with that white robe on," she teased.

He smiled.

"Yeah, he's usually wearing all black," I butted in.

Mrs. Rayas laughed. "The blackest of the black."

"To match the color of my soul," he added. We laughed hysterically.

The event was quite festive. I'd always loved Middle Eastern culture; it is so beautiful as well as family and goal orientated. Everything just seemed to vibe in the culture. I wished I was around something like that.

"Gawt dammit, I don't have a ride home," I remembered as I was helping clean up. Seeing Rani at the door saying goodbye to people, I decided to approach him. "Come here." We walked out into the hallway away from everyone. "Can you please take me home?" I asked with my tiny puppy eyes; I looked like a damn cat!

He smiled and looked around before answering as I pleaded with my huge smile, "You know I would, but we can't do that."

I sighed, "But I don't have a way home-"

Cutting me off, "I want to, but that's too risky."

Frowning, "You're right." He smiled at me, and I smiled back. "Are you about to go?"

Smiling, "Yes," he said. "What are you going to do? Jump in front of my car again?" he said while giggling.

"You must want me to," I said with a smile walking away from him. All I heard was him laughing, and all I felt were his eyes on me. DONT TRIP, I screamed to myself.

Two weeks later.

"Kiesha! Get up off the couch. We have to keep practicing," I said, ushering her to her spot.

"Ugh," she said as she got up.

"This shit is going to be hilarious," Misty said, reading over the script. "This was a good idea, Janee."

Kiesha nodded in excitement.

"Y'all are making me blush," they smiled at me. "We just have to structure it a little more, but we should be all set for tomorrow night."

"PC LIVE, HERE COME THE 'CHEETAH GIRLS'!" we yelled in unison, elated to be a part of our high school's annual talent show this year.

"Well, the generic version, of course," I added. "THE ZEBRA GIRLSSS."

That night, I made sure I brought the blonde wig that Mrs. London loaned me from the theatre club. I was waiting in the back with my mic watching my girls do their thang. Then, there I was walking through the audience. All I could hear was everyone laughing hysterically. I heard Tasha, a lower classmate, the loudest of all. 'What is wrong with her?' I thought to myself, trying not to laugh. I didn't want it to end, but our five minutes were up. The laughing seemed to never end. As we walked to the back where we were secluded from the audience and hidden, I saw something that brightened my night even more.

I smiled. "How'd you like it?"

"I loved it. Perfect, as always." Rani smiled back.

'Awe, he thinks I'm perfect even within all my ratchetness,' I thought.

"Y'all cute," Kiesha added, giggling.

"HA," Misty blurted out.

I straight-faced them both, and Rani just smiled and looked down at his lap.

Deciding to grow some balls, I sat right next to him. He looked up at me and smiled. Kiesha and Misty, noticing what was going on, decided to move down two rows.

Taking his phone out his pocket, "I finally upgraded."

"Ooooou, finally, old man," I teased. There was an awkward silence, and I felt it necessary to try to take his phone. He quickly grabbed my hand, and we both started laughing as we struggled to have our way. While trying my hardest to take it, I accidentally grazed his penis. We looked at each other.

As my mouth dropped, he smiled and shook his head, "Be careful with those hands," he said, pointing at me.

I smiled, then placed my hand on his knee. He turned rosy pink and let a small laugh slip out.

Looking out the corner of my eye, I saw Kiesha and Misty staring at us. I quickly took my hand off his knee, and he looked confused.

"Oop," Misty said, startling him.

"This is even cuter than when he accidentally touched your right tit first semester," Kiesha added with Misty nodding her head.

"That was an accident just like this was," I corrected. Rani nodded his head in agreement.

"Whatever," Misty responded.

"Let us know when we need to prepare to be God mamas," Kiesha added.

Rani and I both glued our eyes to opposite sides of the room, trying to hide our grins.

Three weeks later.

"HAPPY BIRTHDAY!" Kiesha and Misty said, running up to me with a dozen balloons and two bags.

I blushed, "Aw, thank you, guys. I love y'all."

I was greeted with happy birthdays that whole morning. The majority of them were because people had heard others say happy birthday, so they felt it necessary to add themselves to the list. I was finally 17! 17 going on 27, that is.

I walked into class with a big grin on my face. I had my bags in my left hand and my balloons following behind me on my right. I sat down in my seat, waiting for my ass to be kissed on my merry happy day.

The bell rang.

That's right. A bitch was on time that day.

"Everyone settle down," Rani said to the class, talking with his hands, of course.

I snapped my neck, looking back and forth, waiting for the class to settle down, then returned my attention to Rani.

All eyes were on Rani. "Today is a very exciting day, guys," he said.

"IT'S ME AND JANEE'S BIRTHDAY!" Maria, my birthday twin, said.

I looked at her with a big smile, "YAAAAAAAASSS IT'S ALL ABOUT US," I yelled.

Rani laughed and began motioning for us to quiet down with his hands, as the class began saying happy birthday to us.

"That's not good enough, guys," Rani interrupted. "Where is the song? Position yourselves, people," he said.

"Happy birthday to you, happy birthday to you, happy birthday, dear Janeeee and Mariaaaa, happy birthday to you," the class sang in unison.

"AHHHH!" I screamed. "I'm paralyzed with happiness. Thank you."

"Yeah, thanks, guys. That's so sweet," Maria added.

"Oh, but wait, it's not over. We couldn't have a birthday celebration without snacks." Rani pulled a bag from underneath his desk.

He pulled out some Jewish candy, in honor of Maria's heritage, and handed it to her.

"Thank you so much, Mr. Paolini," Maria said.

He smiled, then reached into the bag again and pulled out a cupcake with purple frosting. I loved purple, especially light purple.

Rani handed me the cupcake, "Here you go. I know you like vanilla," he said, smiling.

Ohhhh you know I do, I thought. He thought he was slick with that comment. Tell the truth, shame the devil, babbyyyyy!

"Aww thank you so much," I said.

"You're welcome, ladies. Now, class, today isn't a free day, so pull out Lord of the Flies immediately and turn to page 47."

"Ughhhhhh," everyone said in unison.

Adding to the pain, "Really, Mr. P.! Come on, can we get a break?" Dessy, another classmate, pleaded.

"It's the end of March guys we have a lot to cram in, Dessy you start us off," he said.

Dessy sighed and began reading.

I couldn't believe he had made such an effort to remember my birthday. He'd made it special even when he had to do something for another student too. He always thought so highly of me, and I couldn't describe how much that meant to me. He was always there, and that's all I wanted out of a person. To be there and to see me.

The bell rang.

The class began packing up, "Okay guys, chapter seven is due tomorrow, and there will be a quuuaaazzz, of course," Rani said as people were leaving.

Attempting to walk out the door, he called my name and beckoned me to come over.

He looked to see if anyone else was in the door and pulled something out of his pocket.

It was a stuffed animal- a light purple bunny with big plum eyes. "Here," he whispered, handing it to me.

He stared at me as I admired it, "Awwww," I said, trying not to cry. "Thank you so much."

"Happy birthday," he said, smiling at me.

Time kept going by, and it seemed to bring us closer. I never missed any days of school and stayed after every day as well. He helped me with homework in my other classes and listened to my past and present problems. He laughed at all my jokes and constantly reminded me that being me was okay and especially beautiful. Time was ticking, and it was about to be summer in a little over a month. It seemed like we always wanted to be around each other but couldn't, so we began passing notes. Most of the time, Misty and Kiesha rotated being the messenger. Each note we'd read and then shred. People began noticing even more now; my classmates swore we were married.

Three days later.

I was rushing into Rani's classroom less than five minutes after school with a paper in my hand, "Can you PLEASE help me with my essay for Mrs. Smith's class?" I pleaded. "She's a harder grader than you; Look, she gave me a B on my draft!"

He chuckled, "A B? Really, Janee?" I frowned. "Of course. Are you staying after today?"

"I can't," I whined. "I have an appointment, but I will tomorrow, and I'll email you something special later," I winked.

"I look for-"

Suddenly, two teachers walked in and were so unimportant that I didn't even know their names.

"Hey, Mrs. David and Mrs. Coleman!" He greeted them.

That's what those hoes' names are? Uhmp.I thought.

They smiled and said hello. They quickly turned their attention to me, and one of them took the floor. "Janee, do you have an appointment?" Mrs. Coleman asked.

"No," I responded, confused. Rani tried to hide his confusion as well.

"Well dear, you have to go," she ordered in a condescending tone. I gave her a death stare. "You can't take up Mr. Paolini's time; he has many other students to attend to." Mrs. David nodded in agreement.

"Ok I understand," I said, trying not to be combative. I glanced at Rani.

He gave me a quick smile while they were still turned to me, "I'll see you tomorrow, Janee. And don't forget our appointment after school." I began walking out of the classroom. "I'm always here to help," he continued.

I slowed down to hear if anything else was to be said. I vividly heard Mrs. David say, "Rani, she's becoming a problem. I see her in her all the time."

Mrs. Coleman chimed in, "Is she bugging you?"

"Oh no," Rani quickly rebuked. "She's a great student- a perfectionist actually. She just wants to make sure she stays on the right path. And I'm one of the few teachers she trusts, so I just want to keep it like that."

I could hear their disapproval without seeing the looks on their faces. I guessed we would have to really be on the down-low now. We made our conversations brief and tried to stay away from each other. We took more notes, and he sometimes called me- blocked, of course. He kept reminding me that everything could be different after graduation, and I was okay with that. It shocked me still how much he cared and the sacrifices he made to stay by my side. I would choose him forever.

"So, you're saying that you weren't the aggressor?" Principal Demarco asked.

"No. And I don't know why he would try to blame me for everything and leave out his part," I said frustrated. "Why would he just put me out like this," I said, crying again.

"Well, Mr. Paolini wasn't the one complaining." I looked up in confusion. "Someone else brought this 'relationship' to my attention, and after speaking to him, he revealed the email to me."

It was one of those hating ass, bitch ass, no name having teachers!

"He did, however, add that you jumped in front of his car trying to prevent him from leaving and that you called his parent's house several times," she said.

Oh, so this nigga wants to play.

"Well, everyone knows that it was both of us. People constantly claimed that we were secretly married. Just ask anyone," I said.

She stared at me for a few minutes, "We cannot bring other students into this," she finally said.

"Why not? Misty and Kiesha are the main ones that knew!" I said in frustration.

"Because we can't. And I'll have to do more of an investigation of his part if he even had one." She paused, and I glared at her in anger. "Until then, you are suspended for three days." I gasped. She continued, "For your inappropriate language in this email and confessing to inappropriate behavior such as but not limited to calling his parent's home."

"HE CALLED ME TOO! We used to talk on the phone whenever I didn't stay after school!" I screamed in frustration.

"What proof do you have of that?" she demanded.

"Check the school's phones. I know they record calls." She paused and looked at me.

"Where's your proof?" she asked.

"Ms. Demarco," I started, "have us both print out our phone records." She shook her head.

"I will look into these allegations. But the suspension still stands," she said. "When you come back, we will discuss the future behavior expected all the way up until the end of the year."

Dismayed, I walked out of her office. When I got to the front office, I saw my things- Someone had brought them. I thought back to where everything went wrong. I was just in his classroom until Mrs. Phillips called me down. I wondered why when I got up, he didn't look at me. He was so distant that morning, but I assumed he was tired. Never in a million years did I think he would hurt me the way he did.

Those three days out of school, I cried so hard, and what made it worse was that I was moving to another foster home. Misty and Kiesha were silent because they didn't know what to do. Almost two years, and he would do this to me? I would never have hurt him the way he'd hurt me. My hurt turned into anger throughout the weekend, and I went back to school on Monday with a strong vendetta. He may have won the battle, but I WOULD win the war.

I walked into the conference room in the back of the office with my new social worker, Claire, by my side. I'd told her everything. I told her before everything fell apart, and she understood and had my back 110%.

"Hello," Claire said, greeting Ms. Demarco and my counselor Mrs. Gray. They said hello. I just stared at the wall as soon as I sat down.

"It's good to have you back, Janee," Ms. Demarco said. Mrs. Gray nodded in agreement.

My eyes remained glued to the back wall.

"Well, we spoke to Mr. Paolini. We didn't have many facts, but here's what we have come up with to defuse this situation-," Ms. Demarco started.

Claire interrupted, "What do you mean there are no facts? She's a 17-year-old girl, and he's a 30 something-year-old man!" They listened.

She continued, "If he felt so uncomfortable and thought it was inappropriate, he should've said something a long time ago. But instead, he decided to wait two years later."

"We understand that, but there is a substantial amount of evidence that links to Janee being the aggressor in this situation," Ms. Demarco replied.

"That's because you don't want to go to all the sources and have a scandal in your school." Ms. Demarco paused; Mrs. Gray looked at the floor. "If you guys wanted to find out what really happened, he'd be sitting at this table along with Janee, but he's not," Claire finished.

I stared at Ms. Demarco and Mrs. Gray.

"We want the best for our students here at Hill High School. Janee has shown herself to be resilient, intelligent, and worthy of greatness. We don't want anything to get in the way of that, whether it's herself or others," Mrs. Gray said.

Claire and I listened intently.

Mrs. Gary added, "We feel it is in both JANEE'S and Mr. Paolini's interest not to communicate at all with each other."

My eyes began to water, and Claire let out a sigh.

"Don't you think them not speaking would lead to unanswered questions? Clearly, we can see that they have had a bond for two years," Claire said.

Mrs. Gray looked down once more.

Ms. Demarco responded, "I understand it may be frustrating cutting off all communication, but we feel this is the best way. We have already removed Janee from his English class into another teacher's class that she shares a close bond with as well. It is our belief that Janee will end her junior year successfully this way."

A tear rolled down my eye. And I wiped it quickly. But not quick enough. Claire, Ms. Demarco, and Mrs. Gray stared at me, and I could tell they felt my pain just a little.

Breaking the silence, "Why are you crying, sweetie?" Ms. Demarco asked.

"Nothing," I quickly responded and just as quickly reached into my bag and pulled out the stuffed animal Rani bought me. Everyone stared at it for a good 30 seconds, and then I continued, "Please give this back to Mr. Paolini for me," I reached over and handed it to Ms. Demarco.

She looked at it for a few seconds and finally said, "Why do you think he gave this to you?"

I said nothing as the tears rolled down my cheeks.

Claire chimed in, "What do you think it means when a man gives a woman a stuffed animal?"

After that meeting, Rani and I never spoke. We'd pass each other in the hallways and say nothing. We didn't crack a smile, give a gesture, or even look at each other for more than a second. Kiesha and Misty told me he pulled them to the side a few times and asked them about me. In return, I asked for my essays back. He kept all my essays in his briefcase ever since I'd said he could keep them. They said he was almost upset that he had to hand them over, and that he looked sad a lot and didn't crack nearly as many jokes as he did before. The worst thing they could've done was made us cut off all communication. We were tortured with questions that we didn't get a chance to ask and eventually resented each other.

As I walked down the hallway to my class, I remembered it was the last day of my junior year, and I wasn't excited. I'm never enthusiastic about the summer. At least I could spend it with my girls. And at least I wouldn't torture myself with thoughts of Rani. Who was I kidding? I could never let go.

"Ven aqui, Chica," Mrs. Rayes ushered. I came right over into her classroom. She closed the door, "I know what happened between you and Mr. Paolini." I looked down at the ground, trying to hide the pain expressed in my eyes. "That wasn't right, Chica." I nodded my head. "He shouldn't have done that to you." I quickly lifted my head in shock. "Chica, I went and told Principal Demarco that he played his part as well. It was most definitely 50/50. It was you and him."

I began crying in relief.

I murmured through the tears, "Nothing even happened to him. I got in trouble, and he didn't." She hugged me and said, "No Chica, he got his. He isn't allowed to work at any Hills public schools starting as soon as final grades are entered."

We continued to hug while I cried.

Chapter Seven

MY NAME IS VICTORY!

4:31 p.m. April 22, 2013.

"Make sure you always know the address everywhere you're at," I remember Grandma Sue saying to me before I moved out of my aunt's house. I stamped the address 6529 Westchester Highland Park into my head as I stepped out of the car with my brand-new worker, Sally.

"Janee, welcome home!" she said, beginning to unload the car.

What the hell is this? I thought. I stood there, gazing at a huge mansion-like tan brick building with a large cross on the top front of the house. Is this a lock-up? It's huge. Judge May said they couldn't send me to a lock-up, and she already denied my placement in Children's Village.

"Janee!" Sally called, "are you just going to stand there or help me out?"

I grabbed my chest with all my beautiful purses safe behind a combination lock. That was all I really cared for. Then we both walked straight to the door.

"HI!" a lady screeched as she held open the door for us. I smiled, and Sally spoke. The woman led us to a room with pink carpet, a green couch, and a wooden table. We sat at the table and spent about thirty minutes signing paperwork. I found out the lady's name was Annie; she had a husband named Daniel, and an eight-year-old son named Jaleel. They all lived in the building as well. I met four other girls; I was the fifth to move in. The rooms were small but not so much that I couldn't breathe.

Daniel and Jaleel helped me with my things, and I sat in my room, staring at the wall. I needed to decorate and make the place my own, but I had no money. Sally said my checks would come in a month or so. Every two weeks, I would receive a stipend of $297.73, $150 for rent, and the rest for myself. I would also get a bridge EBT card and be responsible for all my personals. I had a curfew of 11:00 p.m., and I had to maintain my attendance at school. My judge insisted that my worker find transportation to keep me at my original school. My worker was successful, so the next day at 6 a.m. I would be picked up by a transportation service. As my Tío said, "It's a new chapter."

Two months later.

There was a knock at my bedroom door. I opened it to find Annie grinning at me. "Would you like to come to church? You told me you wanted a closer relationship with God a few weeks ago?" I blinked. "I told you my husband and I are ministers, service is just downstairs, please join us."

"Sounds good," I said, closing my door behind me.

They were a different church, and they stood on the statue of people helping people and did just that. Over the next few months, I grew closer to Annie. I rode in the car with her, and we had conversations. We'd eat together and laugh. But she'd sure get on me! See, I had an issue with vindication; I felt God was not needed for that. I could surely handle it. I'd get myself caught up in arguments, one of the girls even slapped me, and in defending myself, I punched Daniel. It was always hard for me to make friends. I didn't do what other people my age did, and when I tried to force it, the repercussions were severe. I was different.

A Woman of Power.

"Man on the floor," Daniel announced before coming up the stairs. That was how he'd let all of us know he was upstairs, and Jaleel would say, "Boy on the floor." "Janee," he called.

"Yes?" I yelled back.

"I need to talk to you. Meet me downstairs in the pink room, sweetie," he said.

"Okay," I answered.

I met Daniel in the pink room and saw him sitting at the wooden table. I sat facing him, both attentive and curious.

"God gave me something Janee," he began.

Huh, what is this man talking about? I paused. See, I'm was not good as this 'God gave me stuff!' I was raised a Jehovah's Witness, and as far as I know, the only thing God gave was threats of Armageddon and watchtowers. "What's that?" I inquired.

"See Janee, I am an apostle, and an apostle is a teacher, a teacher that spreads the word of God to others. God speaks to me, in dreams, through billboards and so on," he said.

"A prophet?" I asked.

"Haha, I have that gift as well," he said. I smiled. "God told me that you would be a woman of power." I blinked in confusion. "Do you know who Kym Worthy is?" He asked.

"No, who's that?"

"Kym Worthy is a powerful woman. She put Kwame Kilpatrick away for the alleged wrongdoings he did to the city of Detroit. She is a powerful prosecutor."

Wow, me? A few weeks later, God spoke to Daniel again and told him that I would hit the six-figure mark. I was apparently destined for greatness. I still didn't believe it. But I intend to fake it till I make it.

Two months later.

There I sat crying in my room after a huge fight with Annie about how I'm combative and that I could leave her home. She always got in my face like I couldn't hear her from a distance. She said that I'm always trying to find more love and stepping on others to do it. I didn't understand or know how I could be the way I was. No one liked me. No one loved me. I just wanted something to hold on to and someone to hold on even tighter.

There was a knock on the door. "Janee, its Daniel. May I come in?"

I jumped up to unlock the door. He entered, and I sat back on my bed.

"Janee, I heard you saying in the spirit 'they don't like me; they talk about me; they laugh at me,' and God is saying, 'but I am going to open up their ears to listen to you.' This seed was planted into you- 'no one wants me I'm not good enough.' It started with your mother. Janee, you have a heart of gold, and that can be very good and very bad. It doesn't matter if they love you at a ten or a two. What matters is that they love you," he said. "Janee, you have to move in this season. God will reveal the time and who to make yourself available to. We all have a purpose and an assignment that will bring people to Christ. But I'm ordered to walk in that purpose, to hear God, for that need of discernment you have to move in God. You have this book you say you have been writing since you were in seventh grade. You never know if that book is how you get your peer's attention or how you develop the confidence needed to love yourself or that deliverance from the seeds planted in you."

That stuck to me. I thought about the message Daniel preached the day before:

He began by asking us, "What are you going to do?"

He assured us that we were not hurting God's feelings if we chose not to move, but asked if we could change naturally without God. Daniel challenged us to ask ourselves, 'what is going on inside of me? Am I going to sit here and do nothing?' He related this restraint to 2 Kings 7: 3-5, "And there were four leprous men at the entering in of the gate: and they said one to another, Why sit we here until we die? If we say, We will enter into the city, then the famine is in the city, and we shall die there: and if we sit still here, we die also. Now therefore come, and let us fall unto the host of the Syrians: if they save us alive, we shall live; and if they kill us, we shall but die. And they rose up in the twilight, to go unto the camp of the Syrians: and when they were come to the uttermost part of the camp of Syria, behold, there was no man there."

"One word, unauthorized, has no place in your future or destiny," Daniel said, "and those unauthorized, disguise themselves to keep us fooled, they operate within a system to gain access. The devil wants to make changes in our lives that aren't pleasing to God. The devil is searching to see how he can bring forth division.

"Solomon (a man of peace) had enemies because the people disliked David. People won't like us because of who we are connected to. The devil knows how to work. These people can get us off course where we could lose access to the worldly system, connected to the famine so we won't be able to move, prosper, and grow. God tells us to keep ourselves distinct, separate, and satisfied.

"Elijah was being blamed for someone else's problem. God promises us prosperity, but it's predicated on what we do! Elijah went to the king of Samaria about Syria, stating that Samaria would win, but it was based on what the Samarian king would do. But we cannot judge folks because we never know how and what God is doing or in what ways he is moving. Thus, we can't be so easily disconnected from people because we don't see what God is doing."

Daniel finished with this, "But Janee, it's time to get up. We can not- we will not sit here and die, or just give up in the famine. The famine signifies those times we wait on God, those 'difficult' times we just don't want to move. But he urges us to keep in our heads, 'Don't die in the famine.' We have to get up and move even when we are reluctant; even when we feel defeated, we have to move."

In Daniel's second closing he magnified the importance of trusting and relying on the Lord. "Trust and keep his commandments. Our next move is predicted on what and how we are thinking. Our mindset must be, 'I cannot become so in tune with sinful folk that their sin affects me.'" In his final closing, he stated that God is willing to move trouble from around us, but we have to move first. God is saying, 'you show Me you're ready to prosper.'

I LOVED IT.

Four months later.

In only a short period of time, I had become a part of the family. I became quite close to Annie's two daughters, Makayla and Camille. Makayla and I bumped heads a lot, and Annie insisted it was because we were so much alike. Makayla told me one week that I was brilliant, and coming from her, I was shocked. She was an upstanding young woman pursuing two degrees and was multitalented. She had it all- the brains, the beauty, and respect. I wished I was like her, and maybe one day I would be. Camille, however, was my road dog. We went to as many places as we could together, but she was three years older than me, so I'd had to miss out on a lot. Camille was always understanding, and she had a gift of connecting with everyone, so she was beneficial to us all in the home. Camille was my go-to person in regards to building and sustaining healthy friendships and body confidence. She taught me how to slip into almost any size and make it look tasteful.

Attending church became the thing to do and was vital in my life. I'd miss church and feel bad about it for days; the spirit of conviction dwelled in me, which meant much change was coming. I did more, I dedicated, I kept my word, and I gave more. Annie taught me how to fast, either by going months without social media or giving up my favorite foods to get that much closer to God. I'd research and keep up devotionals. As time went on, God would reveal the pieces of my life both past and present in dreams. I wrote poetry and kept journals, and happy endings frightened me less. Annie also taught me how to tithe, and sacrifices always accompanied my tithes. The more I gave, the more I was given in return three-fold.

Victory House had become a safe place for trial and error. I lost friends and gained family. I fell out with people and attempted to fall in love with myself. I had failed miserably in the flesh, but as God was breaking me I had gained something precious and priceless, a soul, mind and body that yearned for God.

One year later.

"Wait, wait! Do y'all remember that time Janee took Faith's red dye and put it all on her shoes and clothes?" Annie said after a cackle.

The room, including Jaleel, Daniel, Makayla, and Camille, roared with laughter.

"No, that one time I caught her talking mess and acting a fool while I was getting out the shower," Makayla said.

"Haha! Girl, you were about to drag me out the bathroom, sis," I joined in.

Laughing, "I still can't get over the fact that Janee punched my husband and got away with it." Annie said.

"But wait, mom, how many arguments did y'all get into?" Camille jokes.

"Oooo," Annie exclaimed. We all laughed.

"After the third fight, I just sat down and minded my business because I knew nothing was going down. That's just momma dealing with Janee," Makayla joked.

"I'm going to miss you guys!" I cried.

"Girl, you always crying," Makayla said.

We all laughed.

"You're going off to college; be happy," Annie said.

"Don't ever forget your calling, Janee. Never forget the plans God has for you. They still stand," Daniel said. "God is your Father Janee, use, and speak to Him as such. Keep in mind what Exodus 3:3-8, pointing out verse 6, says, and I'm paraphrasing: I am the Father of your father and his father. I am the father of Abraham, Isaac, and Jacob- I will bless you all as a whole. God has a way of getting your attention. He wants to use you for a great work, no matter where you are. He is what we call Him, and however we may reference Him: Our God, Our father, My God, "My Father, Daddy, Pops, Friend, Family, Savior, Protector, Provider, etc.

If you need to talk, need protection, remember you can call on the Father. The Father will come and intervene, and be there when you need Him. And know that He will answer! Why does God go the long route instead of the simplest route, you may question? But God is a God that deals with each one of us on a different level.

For example, Abraham's Isaac, a type of Christ (sonship) from Father to the Son; everything comes through the Son. Sacrifice things with meaning; God did not take his time, or have an issue sacrificing Jesus. Jacob, Holy Spirit: convictor; will check you! 'I'm not going to let go until you bless my soul.' Wrestling until he encountered the divine: The Father, the Son, and the Holy Ghost. If you want Me, in reference to God, you have to want My Son (Jesus) as well, and the Spirit. God is a mother to the motherless and a father to the fatherless. The God who sees you, God is always ready to provide what you need. Call Him in reference," Daniel finished.

"Amen," we said in unison and laughed.

"And lastly, Nae, do not allow anyone to call you anything but your name!" Daniel urged.

My name is Janee Dukes, your future Judge, a woman of power, and most importantly, a daughter of the King!

Chapter Eight

DEPRIVATION

So, how freaking strange is it to just have someone pop up in your life out of the blue? Saying all the right things and throwing in the most compatible ingredients in order to create the ULTIMATE potion of love. That is until you find out the bottom of the pot has a hole that happens to be very dark, spilling all the powerful forces while binding them together to produce the largest monster of all hate, heartbreak.

"See you," I said to the school transporter, Mr. Sam, as I slammed the black Chrysler van door. Walking into the school, I felt determined! I was going to speak in front of state legislators after school. This would be a great way to start networking in order to become a successful and famous Judge. Kym Worthy, right?!

"Hey, Janee, girl," Alyssa, a lowerclassman, said as I walked through the front hall of the school. After I said hey back, I continued my journey to the café for breakfast. Suddenly I was stopped by a random guy, the moment before I entered the front office hallways.

"You look beautiful today," the young man said while smiling.

"Thanks," I replied awkwardly before he walked away.

Am I being punked?

The warning bell rang for class.

"Let's go, people! Hustle," Mrs. Phillips, one of the hall monitors urged.

"GAWT DAMNIT," I said in frustration.

"Watch your mouth, Miss Dukes! You're a senior now- you must be a good example," she chastised.

"But Mrs. Phillips, I didn't get my bagel!" I whined in frustration hoping for mercy. "Rules are rules," she said, shutting down my pleading.

"LUV YOU TOO MA'AM!" I yelled sarcastically as I walked toward my class.

Ms. Casey was lucky I loved theater. And the fact that I promised my group I would attend class every day that week for our project. I definitely needed that grade to be beyond average. Kill me immediately, I thought. I wanted my bed.

The final bell rang for class.

Ah. Right on time!

Three months later.

Three months after Chris complimented at school, we began talking more on KIK messenger. It turned out we had a lot in common.

"I really can't believe how well you and Chris hit it off!" Misty said. "That nigga loves you."

"Yeah, that's bae or whatever- just please don't tell the whole world."

"Girrrl, you're only two years older than him! Chill out."

"It's not that. I just don't like people in my business- that's how issues start."

"You're right," Misty responded. "Now, can you please help me zip up my dress? And put a smile on your face! It's prom biiiiootchhh," she said, yelling in excitement.

I laughed as I zipped her up.

Love at first sight wasn't ideal to me. To be honest, things like attraction just happen. Or maybe, we find out how beautiful someone is the more we get to know them. We enjoy their company and are attentive to their smiles. We dream with them. And then we somehow live through each other.

The day after prom, May 29, 2014, at 11:31 p.m.

"Did you text Chris and tell him we are on our way?" Misty asked with one hand on the steering wheel and the other holding a lit black and mild.

"You mean, did I Kik him?" I screamed in broken laughter.

"AHHHH, yeah," she said. "You ain't shit."

We arrived quickly at Chris's house. Shockingly, Misty and his brother Eric hit it off just as well.

Opening the back door, I instantly saw Chris and began walking towards him. He smiled at me, "Hey, baby."

"What's poppin', daddy?" I responded.

"That's disgusting," Misty said, walking in. "Now, where's my nigga at, Chris?"

Before he could answer, Eric walked into the kitchen, "Baaaee," he said in excitement. Misty smiled, and they disappeared into the other room.

This was my first time being at Chris's house. I was nervous but still surprisingly comfortable around him.

"I have a surprise for you." I followed him into the basement and saw a pallet laid out. He looked at me, "We don't have to but-"

"It's cool, turn off the lights."

I heard walking, "Um, Janee, where are you?" he asked, searching in the darkness.

"I'm right here," I said, waving my arms as if he could see me. Our hands finally touched. He plopped down on top of me- yes, literally plopped! And I guess the "magic" happened. That was my first time having sex with someone I invited into my body. It wasn't a sexual experience that started with persuasion, or an interest in playing a game. I did not feel I owed anyone anything or thought that I was responsible for providing pleasure because of early stimulation. And for the first time, I wasn't having sexual relations to fit in or to keep another person happy or interested in being around me. I was solely having sex for natural pleasure; I felt normal. Out of all those hands that had been placed on me, his were the only ones I would never scream to get off.

Two weeks later.

It was Misty's open house. She and her family were kind enough to include me in the festivities. Her mom gave us access to her credit card, and let's just say she should've handed it to me rather than Misty.

Walking into the store, "Ahhhh! Misty look!" I demanded, pointing at a dress."

Looking back, "Girl, no! I already told you I found a dress."

Remembering, "Oh yeah."

Glancing to my left, I saw a familiar face, "Misty!!" I screeched, "Kiesha is here!"

Kiesha, Misty, and I ran to each other, "Yaaaaaaaas!! AHHHH!" we screeched in unison.

Looking down at my phone, "Nae, Nae, welcome to the team! I see you and that iPhone," Kiesha teased.

"Yeah, mama let her get on my plan," Misty added.

"Let me start the group chat right away, Kiesha urged.

We smiled.

Later on, during the open house, we managed to slip away from the adults. Misty, Victoria, their cousin Elijah, our other friend Mo, as well as Kiesha and I, rushed into their parent's Buick SUV. You already know where we were headed.

Walking into Eric's house all at once, we were met in the hallway by Eric and two boys that none of us had seen before. As Misty and Eric slid upstairs, the rest of us sat at the kitchen table. The two boys seated themselves on the couch in the living room. They stared at us as we searched for something to discuss.

Victoria sprouted out of her seat and quickly walked to the fridge, "What y'all got to eat?" she called out while investigating their drawers.

We smacked our lips in unison at her foolishness.

Not expecting a reply, "HEAT YOU UP THAT TV DINNER- THAT ALFREDO," Eric yelled out from upstairs.

As Victoria began prepping her food, I thought I'd question the obvious, "Where is Chris?"

Mo hunched her shoulders in confusion.

Elijah looked around, "Who the hell is Chris?" I rolled my eyes. Oh, ma gawwd he's so new, I thought.

Kiesha giggled. "He's her boyfriend, DUH," she said.

Butting into our conversation, "Oooohhh you're his girlfriend?" one of the boys asked as he nudged and chuckled with the other boy.

The first boy would have to have been an inch taller than me, so, 5'8", medium build. He had this buzz cut with a caramel complexion. He wasn't anything special, just looked like an asinine kid.

"I'm Quis," he said, pointing to himself, "and this is Jermaine," he pointed to the other boy. Now that nigga was big, and he had this weird-ass smirk on his face that screamed how annoying he was. I instantly nicknamed him "Kool-Aid man." Ol' funny looking boy. I couldn't believe I was dealing with these boys. Here I was about to enter college and I'm wasting my time entertaining children.

Jermaine waved. "I'm Janee," I pointed to myself, and tapping each person on their shoulder, I said, "This is Kiesha, Elijah, and Mo." They all waved in unison. Pointing at Victoria, "And that's Victoria."

Without even turning around, Victoria called, "What up?"

"Now that we have all been acquainted, let's all look for Chris- everyone should help," Quis insisted.

So, the hunt for Chris began. We split up. Quis and Jermaine went looking outside, as if Chris would be in the bushes or something. The rest of us stayed in the house. One person looked in the basement, one in the garage and the rest between the living room and back porch. I was starting to get really agitated...I don't have a pet so why am I looking for this boy? I thought.

15 minutes later.

Plopping down at the table, "I don't know where this nigga is, but when I find out-"

"We can keep looking if you want," Kiesha offered.

"Let's get to the truth," Quis said, changing the conversation. "Clearly, my mans don't want you- I mean, look at you. I'm shocked and disappointed." Jermaine started laughing.

We stared at him in disbelief.

Kiesha tapped in, "Look here, little nigga boys-"

Elijah, "Nah, I got this, Kiesha! You got us and her fu-" "Let's get it poppin' if you want to," I started. "Take that big ass meatloaf head somewhere else. Ya mama's shit must've been blew out to be able to birth that head of yours!"

"Shut yo fa-" Quis started.

Cutting him off, "I got toothpicks bigger than your dick. You bitches should've been swallowed!"

Quis waved his hands in disbelief, "Mannn, don't let me get to go-"

One, two, three, we all chimed in, making a big fuss. Clap backs flew from left to right and low blows that would definitely leave someone with their feelings hurt.

Startling all of us, "EVERYBODY CAN SHUT THE HELL UP," Chris said, startling all of us.

"Welcome to the party," I said.

Everyone else looked around the room.

Chiming in, "Chris we were just telling her how you don't want her anymo-"

Cutting Quis off with my eyes glued to Chris, "Oh! So you don't want me anymore?"

"I NEVER SAID THAT; GET THE FUCK OUT OF MY HOUSE," he said as he threw a cup of ice water up in the air and attempted to walk away.

I was instantly insulted when I felt water drops hit my right ankle. "Oh, so I need to get out your house? Peace out then. Try that water shit again, Chris; you got the right one."

"Maaannn, whatever. I don't have time for this bullshit," he said after reaching a few steps upstairs.

That night was the beginning of a plethora of disasters. I felt utterly betrayed, and I wanted to know why. Everything had been so great. What changed?

Two weeks later.

"Hellllooooo," I said, answering my phone with one hand and slipping on my sandal with the other.

"Bitch! I'm outside, are you ready?" Misty scorned.

"Coming down now," I responded.

"AN-DA-FUCKING-LAYYY," she rushed. "You know we still have to go pick up Kiesha too!"

"I KNOW. I'm coming." Opening the door and falling into the car, "Wus good, pendeja?" She rolled her eyes.

"You have us disregarded. You know I'm hungry, Kiesha is eagerly waiting, and you know you're ready to see Chris!"

"Okay, but the BBQ doesn't start until noon, and it's 10:30 a.m. This is terrible! You're never on time, but you are for some food." She shushed me away. "Ooooo, bitch! Are you excited to meet their family?" She glanced at me. Gasping, "Ahhhhhh, you are," I said, poking her shoulder.

"Now you know I'm a nigga- I'm for real hungry, and I could use some dick after," she said.

"AHHHHH," I screamed.

So, I had to be cute. I wore this colorful sundress with a yellow tank top to cover my bosoms (I couldn't show what I didn't have! It's a waste of time). I also curled my hair, applied mascara to my lashes, and slapped on about six to ten coats of lip gloss.

"Hey!" the three of us said as we walked into the kitchen.

We saw about 15 people smile and wave to us at once. And the thing is, it was still early!

"Hey girls," a welcoming smile greeted and ushered us to sit down. We sat. "I'm Chris and Eric's mom, Deianne."

"Hey, Deianne!" we said in unison.

"I'm Janee, and this is Misty and Kiesha," I said, pointing to each in turn.

"We are best friends!" Misty added, pulling us all together for a group hug.

"Awe! That's so sweet. Nice to meet you all," she said, smiling. "Let me introduce you guys to everyone!"

Pointing at each person around the room, she introduced us to literally everyone. They were welcoming, and we felt right at home. But even with all these different people communicating with me, I still could not keep my mind off Chris. We hadn't talked much since the incident with his "friends."

Interrupting my thoughts, "Hey Beyoncé! Pretty girl!" Louie, Chris's grandad, said to me. From the corner of my eye, I saw Misty and Kiesha being led to the food by one of Deianne's friends. Misty looked really pleased.

Adding, "She is pretty, isn't she? Deianne said. "Chris was right." She smiled at me.

"Oh, you're Chris's girl?" his grandma asked.

"Yes," I smiled.

"Oh baby, we gotta grill you!" she added with a smile.

Butting in, "Misty is my girl," Eric said, wrapping his arms around Misty while kissing her cheek.

She blushed. In between bites, "Hey babe. There you are."

"You're next!" their grandmother said. They all smiled at me.

I smiled back.

"So what's up, girl?" Louie joked. "How old are you?

"Are you in school? Do you want to go to college?" his grandma asked.

Pausing to see if there were any other questions, I began answering each one, "I am 18."

Interrupting, "Oooooo, Chris got him an older woman!" his grandmother said.

Everyone took their turns "ooooooouuu-ing," across the room.

I giggled, "I have a full-ride scholarship to Western Michigan University."

"Congrats! That's great! Very good," almost everyone said in unison.

"What do you plan on doing?" Louie asked.

"I want to be a judge in the family division dealing with foster care and other family matters," I responded.

Jumping out of her seat, "OHHH MY! Chris! CHRIS!" his grandma yelled. "This girl is about to be a judge."

We all smiled and giggled.

Chiming in, "Your persona and the way you conduct yourself does remind me of Kym Worthy," Roger said.

I blushed. "Thank you."

"Oh yeah, that famous prosecutor! I knew you reminded me of someone," Louie said. "That's really good for you baby."

"How about you, Misty and Kiesha?" Ana asked.

Before I could hear them answer, Deianne signaled me to come over. "Can you go give this Kool-Aid to Chris? He's out there on the porch, and it's real hot outside."

Taking the cup, I turned around to open the porch door. While I was walking out, I heard someone at the table joke, "Don't trip nah! That shit would be embarrassing," while laughing.

I chuckled a little bit.

I handed Chris the cup. He said thank you. Glancing up, he flinched and said, "Oh, hey."

"Hey, C," I answered.

There was an awkward silence as we took turns glancing at each other.

Finally speaking up, "We need to talk," he said.

He got up, and we walked into the kitchen. As all eyes were on us, we tried to ignore the attention and side jokes. We found ourselves back in the basement.

"What's up?" he asked.

"Why are you acting funny?"

"Because… look, you say you want to be a judge, right?" he asked.

"Yeah-"

"Okay, so what's with the petty bullshit, Janee?"

"What are you-"

"You argued with some kids, Janee." I budged my eyes out with my arms crossed attentively. "They aren't nothing. They don't mean anything to you or what you are trying to do and will do."

"I know that-"

"No, man. Obviously, you don't know that."

"Okay, but-"

"But nothing. Let me ask you a question." I listened, waiting. "Where do judges sit in the courtroom?"

Oh, now this nigga is allowing me to answer, huh! I thought. "A raised desk, also known as the bench."

"Okay," he continued after clapping his hands once. Da fuh? Are we playing patty cake or something, because I don't take too kindly to hands moving quickly all in and around my bubble? "So, judges sit higher. And when they are sitting higher, they are in position, right?"

I nodded my head.

"So, act that way. Be the grown-ass, beautiful, smart, and classy woman I love and want to be with."

I was stunned. My arms were still crossed, and he continued gazing at me. Looking around, at the ground, and returning to meet my eyes with his. I had to stop and question myself. Did this nigga just check me?

I liked him, I did. Round two happened that afternoon.

A month and a half later.

The phone rang, and I answered immediately. "Omg, HI!" I screeched.

"HEEEEEEEYYY BESTFRIEND," Misty yelled.

"What are you doing today?" I asked.

"Cut the crap, Nae."

"Girrrrlll. I do not want to talk to Kiesha or Mo. Elijah was right about Mo all along," I whined.

"Okay, but Mo's young-"

Cutting her off, "By a year? Really Misty? Come on."

Continuing, "She is young, and she was just trying to help."

"I don't believe that. When Chris and I were getting serious, remember how I barely wanted anyone to know?"

"Mhm."

"This is why!" I screamed.

"Okay, I-"

"As soon as people get in a relationship and make it all public, then people have everything to say."

Misty remained silent, knowing that my rant had not concluded.

Mimicking, "Oh, he used to always try to touch me and this other girl's breasts. Two months ago, he was trying to talk to me. He made me feel uncomfortable, always trying to touch and feel on me." Continuing in my regular voice, "I HATE THAT."

Finally speaking, "I know you do. Okay, so give you and Mo's relationship some time. Okay?" Misty said.

"Whatever."

"Now as far as you and Kiesha, COME ON NAE!!! We are all best friends."

"Yeah okay but—"

"There's no buts. This is all true. You blew up at her, Janee, and she is so hurt."

"I feel bad for that, I do. I apologized; however, I am hurt as well."

"You both-"

"No, no. Let me finish."

"Okay."

"It hurt me, hearing her constantly speak on someone I love. I would never let anyone disrespect her or you because I love you guys and vice versa."

"Okay, I understand that. You can't really blame Kiesha. She is really just trying to look out for you," she explained. "I'm not trying to step on your toes or overstep boundaries. However, Chris is really changing. I don't know what's up with him, but he is."

Pausing after a sigh, "I know."

Everything started to fall apart. It was weird how things changed. I got so close to Chris's family and was around them all the time with or without him.

I received a text from Chris. It read, "Are you still coming over?"

I replied, "You still thinking about that girl you fingered on the steps in Miami?"

"Chill."

"Nah. You're not shit."

"I told you we needed a break."

"So that means go do nasty shit with girls you don't know? Mama Deianne said you ate her out, actually."

"I didn't eat her out, man! And I've seen her before. Fuck all of that just come lay with me. I'll sneak you in, so it doesn't matter what time you come later on tonight."

"I'm about to get ready for the Birmingham fireworks. I'll talk to you later."

"Alright."

So, Misty, Victoria, Kiesha, our friend Jade and I had finally made it to the fireworks. To be a suburban firework, the place sure was filled with hood rodents! We almost had to fight like three people in the first hour and a half. It was time to cut that outing short.

Slamming the car door, "Okay, who am I dropping off first 'cause I'm really tired?" Misty asked.

"I thought you were coming to spend the night with Eric?" I asked.

Swaying her hands, "Nah, I just-"

Cutting her off, "You just what?"

"Let's just talk about that later, okay?"

"Okay." I was confused. Everything was truly falling apart. Like, when does Misty miss a dick appointment with Eric? Especially because she "loved" him so much. Something fishy was going on.

We are going to fast forward quickly to get to my favorite part of everything, the insanity. That night, Chris and I fornicated all night and in between talked about our issues. The only time we didn't argue was when we were in each other's face. It's almost as if he punished me for not being around him.

Misty went down to Georgia to get a three-week head start at the university since her grades weren't up to par. For weeks, I was on the phone with Eric listening to his love for her and feeling guilty because I knew my best friend was down south playing him. I never understood why Misty couldn't stand being loved by guys. This man really loved her, and she was just doggin him out. Well, while she was doggin him out, Chris was dogging me out too. Trying to keep the peace, I kept myself busy hanging out with my other best friend, Lito. He was a joy to be around, and it was always a plus hanging out with another boy so he could give the tea about niggas. I still kept in contact with Chris's family- they loved me and, surprisingly, he was okay with that.

The telephone rang, and I answered. "Hey, Mama Deianne."

"Hey, girl. What are you doing today?" she asked.

"Nothing at all. Just trying to stay as cool as possible."

"Well, I wanted to get some one-on-one time with you before you head out to Kalamazoo for that one-week water breaker for college."

"I would love that! You know I'm nervous about going."

"You'll do great. So, my cousin is having a birthday gathering at Dave and Buster's. It starts at two! My father and Eric will be there, and I know you love them both."

"Yaaaas, I get to see Louie! That sounds great."

"Girl yes, he loves you! Well, get ready, I'll be there in exactly 20 minutes to get you!"

"Okay, see you soon."

That was a great afternoon. I met a lot of Chris's family. He didn't come because he had been at that dirty nigga Quis' house with Jermaine all weekend. Mama Deianne introduced me as Chris's "little friend," each family member took their turn, ooouu-ing. Louie was sweet enough to pay my bill and drive me home since he only lived a few minutes from me. I loved being around him because he called me Beyoncé and always told me how pretty I was. That's my little boyfriend!

The next day I headed out to Kalamazoo, bag packed and all.

Two hours later, entering a weird sized room with three beds, I was greeted by a welcoming face.

"Hey, I'm Shonda," she said.

Shaking her hand, "Hey girl, I'm Janee." Looking around before placing my stuff down, I settled for the bed right in front of the window.

Trying to make conversation, "This is a weird room."

Shonda answered, "Yeah, this old dusty ass dorm room."

Another girl entered.

Smiling super hard, "Hey guys, I'm Shelby!"

Oh, thank God she's white! I thought, rushing over to her. "Hey, I'm Janee." I always seemed to get along better with people of different races and ethnicities. Sometimes it seemed like black people didn't get me except those closest to me.

"And I'm Shonda."

"Heyyyy," we all said, giggling.

Shockingly, the week turned into a fail. Everyone was arguing like cats and dogs! Two sets of people got into relationships and were caught having sex. One of the guys was arrested because he was 21, and the girl was 17 (how'd she shimmy her ass into college anyway? Oh yeah, late birthday). I almost slapped me a hoe because I got a case of the runs and had to sit out, them one of the orientation leaders said I was pregnant and it spread like wildfire. There was also another hoe destined to be slapped. One chick named Tina made it her duty to insult me.

"Shonda, come sit with me," I waved her down as she was walking toward the rest of the group. She sat.

"You look cute," she said. I winked at her. "Wow, you keep yourself up nice. Always on point. THAT FOREIGN." She added as we busted out laughing.

Butting in, "I don't understand how overweight people can be confident," Tina stated. "Like, you're fat, get over yourself."

"But good sis, please understand that I know SEVERAL niggas that will slap on a bib and eat it with a spoon! Do not be misled," I stated.

She cackled on even after all the clapping and laughing had subsided.

There has been enough arguments and vulgarity in this chapter. I'm assuming from my previous comments and behavior that we can guess what went on next. Back to bae.

Feeling a buzz through my pillow, I woke up to my phone ringing. "Hello," I said, trying to clear my voice.

"Hey, honey! How was your orientation?" Deianne asked.

Sprouting up, "Ughhh", I moaned. "I'll tell you about it when I see you."

"Uh-oh! We can talk at Eric's party tomorrow."

"Yaaaaaas, turn up its E's BDAY."

After finishing my conversation with Deianne, my phone buzzed again. I received a text from Chris. It read, "Baby."

Responding, "Since when am I that?"

"Stop playing with me."

"I'm not. You're confusing."

"I'm going to always love you, Janee. That won't ever change."

"I love you too, C."

"I know. So, are you coming tomorrow?"

"Boy, your brother's birthday is in three days not tomorrow."

"Oh yeah. It's the summer girl, you know I get my days mixed up."

A photo came in.

"CHRIS WHY ARE YOU SENDING ME A PICTURE OF YOUR DICK?"

"You're leaving soon, sooooooo."

A video came in.

"OMG WHY DO YOU STILL HAVE THAT??"

"I'm keeping it forever. It's yummy."

"Byyyeeee, boy."

".... I'm going to miss you a lot."

"Me too. But you know I'll come and visit."

"I wish you could live here."

"Chris, we would rip each other apart."

"Nah."

"I have to talk to you about something when you come."

"What? Tell me now."

"No, in person, Janee."

"Okay."

I wondered what he wanted to talk about. My stomach felt uneasy, and I was very nervous. I HAD TO CALL my friend Lito from a foster care youth group formed by DHHS. HE HAD A PENIS!

"HEEEELURRRR," Lito screamed, answering the phone. "Have you decided to go laser tagging with me and big Esh later on?"

"Yesssss duh! And why do we call Esha that?" I said, cackling.

"It's that or fish titties!" he joked. "I prefer both."

Cracking my neck, "I'M DECEASED!" I screamed. "So, here's the other reason I called."

"Mhhmmmm," he teased.

"Chris texted me saying that he needs to talk to me about something," I continued eagerly awaiting his response.

Choking on some beverage, "He's about to whisk you with that bullshit, guh," he warned. "Finna make you a trifflent ole pumpkin pie to confess dem lies," he said in his best hood rat accent.

"One, you're a rat," I stated, "and two, what should I dooooo, Lito? Please help," I whined.

"Janee, all you can really do is wait and see what he has to say," he insisted.

Murmuring, "I know."

"BUTTTT," he blurted out, "I'll bring the Starbucks vanilla bean shakes so we can talk shit in the meantime," he added.

Gasping, "YAAAAAS."

It was always fun hanging with Lito. He understood and was kind-hearted. Plus, he was bourgeois, just like me.

The next day.

"Your friend, Lito is so sweet," Deianne said, closing the front door behind me. "He could've stayed."

"Oh, no. He has another modeling interview," I bragged. "You know- the lux life," I teased.

"Janee is here y'all," Deianne announced.

I was welcomed with every greeting uttered.

"Oooohhh, look what we have here," Louie started.

I smiled at him with my best smile.

"That's my girl!" he said. "How are you, baby girl?"

"I'm great! How are you?" I asked, greeting him with a hug and kiss.

Out the corner of my eye, I saw Eric, "HAPPY BIRTHDAYYYYY," I screamed.

"Thank you, sis," he said as he reached for a hug.

I began engaging in conversations with everyone present and was suddenly interrupted nearly moments after by a tap on the shoulder.

"Hey," Chris said as he embraced me with a hug.

"Hey C," I said, hugging him back.

"Aw shit!" but in Eric. "He's blushing and shit."

All eyes were on us as usual. We both started smiling and quickly moved on to other conversations with the people in the room.

Twenty minutes later, I noticed Chris left. I refrained from allowing my eyes to wander. While trying to focus on something else, I received a message from him:

"Come here. I'm in the basement," it read.

The conversation wasn't at all like I thought it would be. We found another thing in common, our past childhood. I was no longer perfect to him that night. I told him all the things I never said. He never interrupted or really said anything until I paused. He remained attentive throughout, and his eyes softly kissed my scars. He cried out to me the pain he had been hiding for so long. And I watched him slowly fade away as each memory emerged out of his mouth. I could not take my eyes off of him even when the conversation ended, and we attempted to laugh it off with a Netflix movie. I fell in love with all he had to offer- his ugly, his grace, and his truth. Through the torment of egregious thoughts, words, and actions- I was wanted, I was safe, and I was loved. Comfort landed in time for all the battles to come.

Chapter Nine

FIGHTING ON FOR WHAT?

Part 1: "THROW YO HOOD UP"

More often than not, we do things when people say to do them because it is considered common or because we choose to go beyond good judgment. Situations like this are hellish, but after they have passed, they certainly become one hell of a story. Tell me what is worse, helping someone fall apart or knowing that they are falling apart and doing nothing about it?

Walking into room 218, Karol Hall, I saw a fair toned girl with big curly hair. She had to be about 5'8 in height, and I assumed she was my age. This must be my new roommate for this school year, I thought.

Noticing me out the corner of her eye, "Oh my God!" she proclaimed. "Hi, I'm Skylar."

Smiling, "Hey girl, I'm Janee."

"Nice to meet you," we both replied.

Skylar had what I called a "Bill Cosby Family," all of her immediate family members came to support her. They decorated her room with detail; I noticed she loved turquoise. While they helped decorate and organize, I took multiple glimpses of them- they were all elated.

Fifteen minutes later.

"Hey, Janee," Skylar tapped on my shoulder to get my attention. I smiled at her.

"My family and I are going out to eat. I'll see you later," she said.

"Ok, have fun," I replied, smiling. I could've guessed that was coming next. 'More family bonding,' I mocked in my head.

"Hey, we are going out too, don't worry," my worker Kathrine assured.

Kathrine cleared her schedule to make sure I was comfortable at Western. She moved all my things upstairs (she spoils me) and attempted to help decorate the little space. She and Sandy were the best social workers I'd ever had.

Later that day, I ran into familiar faces.

"OMG! Hey girl, hey," Shonda screamed. She and Shelby jumped me with hugs.

"Hey y'all," I said, elated to be seeing them.

"Yo, what's on for tonight?" Kiara crept into the conversation, and we all re-hugged.

"The Alphas are having a party," Shelby said.

Chiming in, "You would know about these black parties' child!" Shonda teased. "We have to name you a ghetto name."

Laughing, "I told y'all I wasn't white inside."

We all laughed.

"Aren't the Alphas them niggas that shimmy?" I asked.

They all burst out laughing.

"THE KAPPAS," they screamed in unison.

"They're all dancing and wailing niggas to me," I replied.

We started walking towards the door to explore the campus- the journey had just begun.

Later that night, Shelby, Kiara, Paris, and I decided to explore as many campus parties as possible. Unfortunately, Shonda couldn't join us because the turn-up swayed her another way- We hoped to meet up with her later. We all looked good. Kiara had on this cute dress with a slit, Shelby had on some boogie shorts that made all the niggas holler, Paris had on a slimming dress with her hair pinned up, and I had on a long beautiful sundress with a slick wing liner and some hot pink lipstick. It was Saturday night: let the hoeing begin.

"I am pisssseedddd yall!" Kiara screamed.

"Come on now, sis, this isn't the first time black girls have been denied at the door," I said through a chuckle.

"But for real, I'm white, and they wouldn't even let us in," Shelby joined in the complaining.

Paris chimed in, "I'm like, so annoyed because the white frat parties BANG!" she whined.

"WHO CARESSSSSS," I whaled. "We are in college, we have no curfew, let's find somewhere else to turn up! The night is still young!"

Twelve minutes later.

"Welcome to Wendy's, how may I help you?" a friendly voice asked.

"Hey, can I get a small Baconator with a medium vanilla frosty?" I asked as I finally reached the front of the Wendy's line.

"Sure, is that all?" the cashier asked.

I nodded.

After waiting five minutes for my food, I sat at the table where Kiara, Paris, and Shelby were already seated.

"That's all you got?" Shelby asked with fries damn near pouring out of her mouth.

"Yes, bitch. I'm not the one who's high. I just giggle-"

Cutting me off, "Just a little bitch, get it right," Kiara said, geeking my head up.

"I concur," Paris chimed in after a few gulps of Coca Cola. He burped and said, "So guys, there's a 7-Eleven across the street."

We all nodded. "We should totally get drunk- like six shots of Crown Royal a piece."

"Oh, hell no. This bitch is trying to kill me," I fussed.

"I'm in," Kiara and Shelby said in unison.

Paris smiled while I shook my head.

Eight minutes later.

"FINALLY," Shelby screamed in excitement as she poured Kiara and Paris a drink.

Taking a sip, they started coughing.

"See, that shit is too much," I complained.

"Just take a sip," Kiara convinced.

"I've already caught a contact just watching y'all drink," I said.

They laughed.

"You can't catch a contact that way, Janee," Paris corrected.

Chiming in, "Yeah, that's only with weed or crack- one of the two," Shelby said.

"I'll remain the designated walker and enjoy watching y'all act crazy," I giggled.

"Ayo bitches."

We all looked around in different directions.

"Yes, you hoes."

We looked across the street and saw a black man yelling and waving an 1800 bottle like it was a flag on the Fourth of July.

"What the fu-," Paris started.

"What type of foolish-," I began.

"He got us fu-," Kiara began.

"Fuck him, I gotta pee," Shelby said. We all laughed.

"Ay y'all," a dude said, scaring us.

"Sorry ladies, I'm Luke, I go here too. I saw y'all at Wendy's."

We introduced ourselves.

"Where are you all headed to?" he asked.

Pushing us out the way, "Well, I'm tip-tip-up-syyy, and I gots ta pee," Shelby said.

"AYO STUPID BITCHES," the man across the street yelled.

"YEAH, YOU HEAR US, YOU DUMB HOES," some woman yelled.

We all stared at them in disbelief.

"Oh, they on that good shit- shits crazy," Luke said.

Whispering, "Yall, he got a whole tribe with him," I said.

"All them niggas over there looking like Bebe's kids from up tha block," Shelby whispered back.

Paris, Kiara, Luke, and I paused, staring at her.

"Let's let her slide, she's drunk and harmless," I said.

"I'm gonna try to walk y'all, but I have to meet my friends up the street at this one store," Luke offered.

"Thank you!" I said. "They are so drunk."

He laughed.

We started walking, and the group continued to yell from the other side of the street.

"Just ignore them," I said, sensing the other three girls getting heated.

The group continued to yell obscenities.

"FUCK YOU DUMB AS BITCHES," Shelby started.

I tried to shush her.

Kiara interrupting, "Triff ass black bitches."

I shook my head.

"LIKE, SAY THAT TOUGH SHIT TO OUR FACES," Paris continued. (Paris was such a valley girl).

"Y'all got to chill," I said. Luke and I attempted to calm them down.

The group started walking towards our side of the street.

"Y'all, there isn't a bathroom down here. It's three a.m., and the other stores are closed. Let's just go back to the dorms," I suggested.

"Yeah, y'all, Janee is right. Plus, I'm already close to where I'm meeting my boys at," Luke added.

"No, no, no! There is one down here," Shelby fussed.

We continued walking, and Luke left shortly after we reached the nearby gas station. It was closed, of course.

"Seeee, let's go," I suggested, seeing the group getting closer, still screaming at us.

This banshee with Flocka hair eased up on me. Shocked, I glared at him and said, "Hello, I am trying to find a suitable restroom for my friend."

Chiming in, "That's me, hoe," Shelby yelled.

That comment summoned the whole tribe, and they started going wild, preparing for war.

"Shut up!" I yelled at her, reaching for Kiara. "Look sir, my friends are drunk. I'm just trying to get them to safety."

"Bitch, I don't care! I want that bitch," he screeched, pointing to Paris.

"Wellllll I DON'T want you, BIOOOTCH," she hissed.

Ah ma gawd. The chief began approaching her. "Okay, let me call the police," I said.

Flinging from in as if from a vine "Ay hoe. I'm 25; you can't call the police on me!" another man said.

"Okay, I'm just trying to get-," I started

"BITCH YOU HEARD HIM," a girl said, approaching me. I know this thang better get out my face, I thought.

"My bro wants at them hoes-" she started. I gently placed my arm in between us, "Look ma'am-"

The beast arose and popped me on my forehead.

"JANEE NOOO," Kiara screamed as I popped and dipped her face.

The next thing I saw was all fifteen (six being boys) pulling my hair. The initial guy burst an 1800 bottle over my head while another pulled my halter-top down and poured liquor on me. I stood my ground as I was being swayed back and forth, feet glued to the ground. I glanced over and saw none of my friends do anything. Instead, a Caucasian frat across the street laughed and cheered it on. I saw cars riding past laughing and continuing on. I looked crazy, and once again, I was alone.

Part 2: Bill Cosby and Them

After a winded first day, I ran back to my dorm from classes and decided to clean up. I had already invited Shelby and Shonda over so we could get something to eat after. I was instantly pissed when I noticed my things had been slightly moved (I noticed everything). Skylar and I made it clear that we would never move each other's things, so I was shocked. Looking at her side, she definitely had more space for me to have more things than her. I decide to move my things back into the little space I had available. In doing so, I moved her refrigerator over slightly to provide a spot for my make-up box.

Interrupting my organizing, Shelby and Shonda entered. "WAZZZUPPP," they said in unison.

"Heeeyy," I said, waving.

"Girl, I love your confidence," Shonda said

"Yeah, I know right. Look at you all naked and free," Shelby added.

I winked at them both. We started off with a good hoe conversation until we were interrupted by the sound of the door opening. Skylar entered with her best friend, Asia, and we all greeted each other. Continuing our conversation as I'm getting dressed, Skylar interrupted.

"Hey Janee, why did you touch my stuff?" she asked.

"I just moved over your fridge so I could put my make-up box right there," I answered as I pointed to the small space.

"Yeah, but-" She started.

"You have less stuff but more room than me, I just wanted that small space," I interrupted.

I could see Asia, Shonda, and Shelby's eyes following the both of us; all they needed was popcorn.

"If your stuff wasn't so huge, you could make more space," she said.

"Careful, I will slap that two-hours-a-day application of what you call make-up right off your face!" I warned.

"You're threatening me," she replied

"Now you know good and well I'm giving you my word," I said, stepping up into her face.

"You are so fat and miserable," she said, "no wonder you got jumped." Shelby, Shonda, and Asia quickly jumped up to get in between us. I continued approaching. "The only reason you're here is because you're in foster care and steal all the tax dollars," she screamed. Here she goes again with the foster care jokes, I thought. I kept walking up on her, trying to shove all of them out the way. "My parents-" she began.

"Girl, shut up. Your parents are my parents since they are contributing to all the tax dollars I get. Now I'm a Cosby too!" I taunt, almost slapping her with my left tit as I was still naked. "Get this bitch out my face." I shook my head. "You are moving out anyways, why are you talking to me?"

She and I went on a screaming match, and after about seven minutes, our friends broke it up with Skylar storming out of the room.

"Now I want to know why she had to bring up foster care," Shonda said, swaying her finger in the air.

"Because she's a bitch," Shelby said before I could answer.

"Well, I'm a bigger one...literally," I said, throwing in a pun for a good laugh.

Laughing, I pointed Shelby to her three drawers. "You said you needed clothes, right?" I asked.

"Haha, yeah," she answered.

"Well, welcome to Plato's Closet on Skylar's dime. Help yourself," I urged.

"I AM SCREAMING," Shonda said and burst out laughing.

A few days later, Skylar and I met with the hall director, Meg, and decided that it would be best to switch roommates immediately instead of in two weeks. Quickly after even more rumors spread from dorm to dorm, I was officially Skylar's bully. Apparently, that time I actually beat her up! No one dared to ask my side of the story. Skylar conveniently left her faults out. Back to the label bully. My voice was always too loud to ever be considered a victim.

Well, at least I had a roommate and a friend. Shelby has blessed the building!

Part 3: Never Too Much Pain

"Dude, how mad was Chris when he found out?" Shelby asked. "I heard him screaming over the phone."

"Girl, he wasn't screaming at me. He was upset that I didn't tell him right away," I answered. "Deianne told him. I begged her not to."

"Oh yeah, didn't she say she would try to come and visit you?"

"Yes, but Chris has school, and she and Eric work as well," I answered. "So, I'm going to try to visit them whenever I can."

"Hey!" Shelby screeched, "I have an idea. You know my boyfriend, Max? I know y'all haven't met yet, but you guys will soon."

I nodded my head.

She continued, "Well, I want to go visit my brother in Detroit, and you said Chris lives in Farmington. We can just take you when we go!"

"Oh my God! Really?" I screamed. "That would be perfect!"

"I know right, I can't believe I didn't think of this sooner!" she said. "I'll double-check with Max, but we should go in two weeks."

"That's perfect, I just got my refund, and I'll have another SIL check Friday! I'm excited."

Frowning, "I still haven't gotten my refund or my check. I hate Yvac. Do you mind if I get a few things? You can just put the stuff from here on out on to a tab!"

"Sure, no problem!" I said.

At the mall.

"I can't believe you're starting Christmas shopping so early," Shelby said.

"I can't pass up a good deal, and plus, I want to give everyone their stuff early. You offering to take me to see Chris made me think I should just give everyone their gifts early." I said. "I have everything planned out."

"Oh yeah you do! $900 on gifts!" she said, "You are so cool, dude. I really appreciate you." Handing me a few outfits, "I think I'm going to get these," she said.

Grabbing them, "Great choices. Now, let's head out so we can get ready for tonight," I said.

At Victory House, Greater Divine Resurrection Church of God in Christ introduced me to Luke 12:48, "But he that knew not, and did commit things worthy of stripes, shall be beaten with few stripes. For unto whomsoever much is given, of him shall be much required: and to whom men have committed much, of him they will ask the more," and I felt because I was given so much that it was my job to give to others. Glory to God, nothing is solely ours.

Shortly after, I discovered no matter how genuine our intentions, expectations would surely overkill it all. Friends would turn into enemies, and those we called our family would do a complete 180. You'd think after giving your long, hard-earned youth to one young man that he'd cherish it forever. This toll left me with a lot of nothing and so much of everything. The trails that led me to him were now scattered among the fields of my growth. Distancing me from what was and what is. You could only wish that his family would approve of you and the love and respect you had quickly gained for them all. But everything changes when you say no. Everyone starts moving funny, and next thing you know, you're back from your long winter break of ignoring responsibilities, drowning in intercourse, weed brownies, and not a care in the world regarding your future. How blissful this all sounds until you're back at Western waking up with your wrist covered in dried up blood, half of it on your skin, and the other half on the bathroom tile. Oops, I did it again, fight on alright!

"Janee!" Shonda screamed, jumping to my rescue. "You have to stop doing this shit."

"It doesn't even matter. All that matters is this little crazy will be busting jokes about it twenty minutes from now," I said, referring to myself.

"It's not funny. What happened?" she asked.

"Oh, the same old, same old," I said.

"Chris? What did that shithead do this time"? she asked.

"Nothing, that's the thing. When we talk, it's nothing. I guess because his mama left me alone he figured he should do the same," I said.

"What did you even do? I'm so confused," she asked.

"She claimed I was walking around with an attitude. But I told her a bitch like me is severely depressed, and I enjoy cutting my wrist until I giggle again," I said, smiling while wrapping my arm in gauze.

I wanted so badly to find an answer- a letter, note, or a poem that was not meant to be read. Something that wasn't meant to be heard. Then I realized, she had morphed everything that she wanted it to be in her own mind. She decided to do any and everything to dismiss any form of reconciliation, therefore canceling the love and care that had existed before.

"Again, not funny. Well, that's not a valid excuse," Shonda said.

"That's what I said, but you try telling it to that stubborn lady. Yo, she broke my heart- worse than Chris. She was like a mom."

"Yeah, I know you guys were really close."

"Yeah, yeah, yeah," I said, walking out of the restroom.

"Wait," Shonda yelled. "Another academic letter came- I didn't mean to invade your privacy, but it says you are on probation. Janee, you have a .68 GPA. You could lose all your scholarships."

"At this point, they can take all that shit, just leave me a few bottles and I'll be on my way," I yelled back.

Crazy is what crazy does; I had no fight in me.

"Here, take a nap," Shonda said, handing me my favorite throw and closing the door on her way out.

I waited until I heard her footsteps drift down the hall, then I opened my eyes and saw the sun trying ever so earnestly to slide its way into a glimpse that was meant to lay heavenly over my face. I then realized the love and endearment Chris and his family had once in their hearts, never existed. I was awake then. I closed my eyes once more to see clearer, and there he was, standing tall, absorbing all light and fully hovering over my greatness. Refusing to release its captivity, only to let it be released when he decided to water the seed that was always apparent. He was unwilling to dislodge his hold, and control over it all: my self-esteem, my courage, and my décor. Only to nurture it and then eventually breach it's meaning, to perturb the nature of its emanation. I was still not free.

Two months later, at 7:45 p.m., I tried to reach out again, a simple 'I love you' text. Nothing back. She probably didn't even read it. Two hours later, at 9:45 p.m., I was filled with 95 singly sorted mixtures of pills, a half cup of Listerine, a cap of bleach, and 25 cuts on my arm.

When I cut, I wrote:

Fill your ears with music and sing while your demons guide you, and then you'll really feel nothing. Various musical sounds seem to numb the pain and afflict the motion. Whether horizontal or vertical. Each note surfaces a cut, and every other beat encourages a slice. Trying to surface the blood, frustrated because I was looking to be rescued, but as I glanced up, I found no one. So I continued, becoming my own worst enemy, sabotaging all my accomplishments while altering my mind. I looked up once more and saw no one. I was officially lost. I gazed off while I awed over what I had just created. Lines are art. The way they trail off and drip to mark a new pain. And then dry up, providing a new path, to recollect every painful memory. Some people aren't worth saving.

By 11:02 p.m., I was being rushed out of Karol Hall by an emergency crew. They had found me in the hall passed out, with everything I consumed right there by my face. I died for 32.5 seconds and cried when I woke up.

The day after, I found myself on the phone with my campus coach, Kelsey. She told me that my full-ride scholarship was taken away and that if I wanted to continue my education at the university, I'd have to exceed my loans. Two weeks later, the day after my birthday, I left campus. I lost my boyfriend, a family, friends, and my scholarship. The crazy thing is, I still didn't care

Chapter Ten

ME VS. ME

It had been about two months since I'd returned home from Western. I had to admit it felt much better being in the presence of the Lord as well as others that follow Him. My stomach was healing, and I was able to sleep better at night; however, I still didn't know what I'd woken up to.

The lobby had a weird smell and feel; I could sense abandonment. I could feel pain. Anxiousness rumbled in between each tile, and a few people were afraid. I was always uncomfortable with what I could relate to.

"Janee Dukes," called a woman with a smile from the doorway. I quickly got up and followed her with the door closing behind us.

We stopped at the fourth door to the left, and I read, "Tara Cook," on the door.

The lady smiled at me and said, "We are so happy you decided to seek care with us. Your therapist's name is Tara, and she is excited to meet you." She opened the door, and a smile greeted me from beside a desk.

"Hello, Janee! It is a pleasure to meet you," she said, shaking my hand. I stood anxiously. "Please sit down anywhere you'd like," she continued.

I sat. "Thank you," I said, relieved.

"So Janee, first, I think it would be most appropriate and beneficial to start out by telling you a little bit about myself," she said.

I nodded, allowing a half-smile. Oh great, I get to hear a story about her awesome childhood filled with three bad days- all because she couldn't get her self-entitled way, I thought.

Smiling, "Great well, I am 32-years-old. I was raised by my grandmother for ten years due to my mother and father abusing drugs. After a few mishaps with other family members, I was placed into foster care. I remained in foster care until I was eighteen years old. I decided to leave voluntary foster care before twenty-one due to an excessive amount of sexual abuse by the male staff in my group home. Eager to succeed, I pushed my way into college at U of D Mercy. There I studied Psychology with a minor in Criminal Justice. It took me six years to graduate with my bachelor's, but I did. Shortly after, I went back to that same group home to be an in-home therapist to the youth for five years, sadly, that home was shut down, and I then transferred here. I have been working here now for three years! I am currently engaged and live in metro Detroit." she said.

I didn't know how to respond.

"Not your typical entitled therapist, huh?" she joked. "I attempted to cut the story down to save time, so pardon me if it's vague. If you have any questions, I am an open book!"

"You were in foster care?" I asked.

"Yes! And according to your files, you are in foster care. Looks like you were raised by a grandparent as well," she said. I nodded. "Well, it sounds like we have some similarities." I smiled.

"I realize it's ignorant to assume; however, you seem lost for words, Janee," she said.

I began gazing at the floor again. The tile was perfect, and the pattern simple. How can things be both perfect and simple?

"Janee," she called.

I looked up.

"Why are you here?" she asked.

Taking a deep breath, I answered, "I intend to touch base on everything no one talks about when it comes to experiences I have had and am having. Anything sickening that pops into my mind, anything unruly or devious, I won't hold back. They say the insane are bold and injustice- I want to see how real I can be. See, people will pierce their ears with profane language, bulge out their eyes for nudity, and claim to be the realest of them all. Let's find out how raw and uncut we can get and handle. Let's talk about and say the things that no one ever says."

"Is that what you think of yourself?" she asked. "An insane person?"

"My name is insanity, and I wouldn't have it any other way."

"What does this word 'insanity' exactly mean to you?"

"To be aware, wise, and used. To be present, restless, and sensible. To be all these things while persevering through the pain. Insanity is unconquerable."

"Well, I am certainly excited to get this healing process started with you," she said as I nodded. "Such wisdom for a nineteen-year-old."

"More like such pain for a nineteen-year-old," I responded.

She chuckled. "But you see, my dear, that's where the wisdom comes from."

I smiled.

I did not know what I had in store with this therapist, but I had a really good feeling as always. I was ready to get the help I'd been yearning for; however, this was all predicated on me. I knew there's a lot of pressure out of nowhere. Some of the pressure I did recognize. However, I was certain that I was ready to be healed.

One month later.

"Describe yourself," Tara said.

"Definitely not ugly but far from pretty," I responded.

"Now, how does that make any sense, girl?" she asked.

"I am not pretty like my family, or this world wants me to be, but I'm not ugly where I would ever be a meme," I explained.

"What type of pretty did your family want you to be?"

"I am heavy set, burnt caramel skin, almond eyes with a round face and wide nose in the center. I have no shape of a butt, and my breasts are purely an illusion. My skin is overly sun-kissed, so I missed out on that glow. I have scars, cuts, and scraps all down my left arm. My voice is not becoming nor sweet. It is raspy but also somehow rich," I described.

"All those things sound pretty beautiful to me. I don't know, Janee. Maybe your family is either blind or crazy," she said through a chuckle. "You are brilliant, strong, and able."

"That may be true to you, but all I know is everything I do involves strength, and I believe my strength in all things has made me weak in everything."

Two months later.

"How is therapy going?" Annie asked as I walked through the front door. "I really liked attending your session last week. Tara seems so genuine, and she knows the Lord."

"It's really awesome, Mom. She has helped me find the right medication and the correct milligrams. She helps me cope when I'm not on my medicine, and she constructs great worksheets for when she's away. She's almost a match of a blessing like you and Dad," I said.

After falling, you'd think I'd have decided to make a bigger change sooner than later. Well, they don't call me crazy for no reason, you know ya girl had to bump her head and get run over and break a few more times to attempt to get it right. Anyway, here's day one, I am celibate, I will refrain from cursing, and I will eagerly run to God. Let the tests begin!

Having a strong and positive support system would help me obtain the goals that God had set forth for me. He had my whole life figured out, and although He revealed glimpses of my future, I still doubted. I mean, really. A woman of power, what does that even mean? I'm trying to make it all conquerable in my mind as to how and why He would ever intend me to exceed a 4.0? In high school, I was a 2.89 shorty, just trying to make it. And don't even get me started on this wave of income that He had promised me and a prophet's reward. Of all these prophecies, I can't seem to get this one out of my head, and that's the purpose of writing a book about my life. I am in no way a former prostitute that got off of drugs and found the Lord. I wasn't sex trafficked; I have no memorable, strong testimony. So how can he use my words? I absolutely fail at comma placement, and my speaking abilities are depleting. What use am I?

"Now Janee, what is this foolishness you have written?" my aunt Candance asked. "I just saw this text and nearly slid off of 94."

"Oh no, Auntie, don't do that," I said. "Auntie, I'm lost, and I'm worthless. I am perplexed as to what my purpose is. What do all these things mean?"

"Baby. It is not our job to know all that God is doing and what He has done. It is only our job to follow and listen to God," she said. "Listen and be willing to do His will. The answers may come later, or they may never come."

That wasn't good enough for me. Three days later, I found myself bugging my father Daniel about the same matter and two weeks after that, questioning my mother Annie as well. They all said the same thing. Oh God, oh God, what do you want from me?

The voices slipped in, prepared to swindle me into confusion. You cannot possibly fulfill His will. You are not equipped for the journey.

I answered, "Well, duh, I know this. I'm worth-. You know what, I'm not doing this with y'all today! Let's challenge that-"

But your self-esteem stops you from everything. It breeds envy and jealousy. At times you are possessive and unruly. Your low self-esteem is you, they interrupted.

I paused and thought of a podcast I listened to by Apostle Gabriel McCullum. It talked about being equipped for the journey. He used Acts 1:6-8, "When they therefore were come together, they asked of him, saying, Lord, wilt thou at this time restore again the kingdom to Israel? And he said unto them, it is not for you to know the times or the seasons, which the Father hath put in his own power. But ye shall receive power, after that the Holy Ghost is come upon you: and ye shall be witnesses unto me both in Jerusalem, and in all Judea, and in Samaria, and unto the uttermost part of the earth." Apostle McCullum pointed out how burdensome it may be to be unable to see where we started and all that we have advanced to where we are now. In all of this, if we were not equipped for the journey, the Lord wouldn't place us in specific areas. Thus, I was there for a reason. In response, I challenged every thought that came up against the will of God.

My mind was consumed with the power to acknowledge what God was willing to give me. However, at times, that doubt still lingered. The voices were distant, but I still needed to consult with Tara. She and I had become extremely close. I trusted her and believed she was sent by God. Maybe she could help me lay out some of my difficulties.

Two days later.

Walking into Tara's office, I saw her smiling at me beside the door, ushering me to sit down. There on the desk was a bottle of water, pretzels, and a cookie- she knew me so well.

"Janee, I am so happy to see you. I truly love our sessions," she greeted.

"I love our sessions as well, Tara. You have been helping me so much!" I said.

She smiled, "As I said two weeks ago, this session will be short, but I had to fit you in before I leave for my vacation. I have printed out worksheets for you to do if need be. And of course, if there is an emergency, my personal cell is open to use. Our little secret." I smiled.

She got up and pulled out a pink folder with my name on it from her bookshelf. She then sat back down and reached over the desk to hand it to me.

"Here you are, my dear," she said.

The first paper read:

Turning strengths into weaknesses; reversing triggers. Take your power back.

After my therapy sessions, about five hours later, I found myself severely distraught over who knows what, I guessed the Prozac wasn't working. Thus, I began to fill out the sheet.

This assignment reminded me of Philippians 3:13-14,

"Brethren, I count not myself to have apprehended: but this one thing I do, forgetting those things which are behind, and reaching forth unto those things which are before, I press toward the mark for the prize of the high calling of God in Christ Jesus."

Step one: Discover what sets your emotions off. What are your triggers?

- Acceptance/inclusion
- Consistency
- Intimacy vs. sex

Step two: Explain your connection to these triggers. How did they come about?

- When I was a child, my mother left. I never felt I was good enough for anything or anyone; this deeply affected my self-esteem and self-worth. I have been searching to be included everywhere, no matter where I am in life, I search to be included and accepted. At times, I have struggled with not being good enough, and thus, no one else was. I measured the amount of love each individual had for me. And my loyalty and time leaned towards the ones that loved me the most or seemed to even for a short amount of time. What is love? I have so many expectations.
- Change has always frightened me. It usually meant someone was about to leave, or peace would end. When I don't feel consistent, whether in my life in general or within relationships, I panic. Something bad is going to happen.

- I find it difficult to form any type of relationship, let alone one that includes sex. During the younger years of life, I was introduced to sex by several relatives and a few family friends. When connecting to people, there is a pressing need to give my all to them. This need is made up in my own mind. I don't feel secure if I haven't given all of myself in relationships. And after I feel at my lowest. I'm most comfortable with this feeling. I don't know how to have meaningful relationships with the opposite sex while sex is involved, whether through interaction or conversation. What is life without pleasing?

Step three: How will you stop these triggers from consuming you?

- God has spoken, "They will never understand you, so stop attempting to make them do so." I hear myself saying in the spirit, "They don't like me," but God is saying, "They will listen to you." I am different, and everyone doesn't get to enjoy my presence or to have a deep connection with me. And like the apostle said, "It doesn't matter if they love you at a two or a 10, all that matters is that they love you." Accept myself, include me within myself, and others will either follow, or some won't matter at all. I will always be enough.
- The thing that frightens us most is probably the next thing we should do. Change is always good- it can mean a promotion or a demotion. I can't let the 'what if's' and how come's' hold me back. The only thing that is constant is change.
- I don't have to give my all and my whole self to prove that I love people. The minimum will be enough, and I can save my whole for those that God guides me to share with. Giving my all to everyone sets me up for failure and heartbreaks due to unmet expectations. Not everyone is like me, and those that prove to be genuine MAY deserve my all. My minimum is enough.

I was doing the homework. I was putting in the effort. I was pushing. I was no longer a crazy girl. That was the time to heal, do all I could, and be still knowing that He is God.

Five days later.

"You know, Janee, I never hear you speak much about friends," Tara said.

"That's because I don't have any. The people of my generation do not understand me. I'd rather hang out with their parents and grandparents than them," I chuckled.

"You are quite wise," she said. "But whatever happened to your friends from high school? Kiesha and Misty? And then also Kimmy, your childhood friend," she asked.

"Want to start with truth or deep?" I asked.

"Aren't they one and the same?" she asked. "Deep."

"Okay. Kimmy: one of the gentlest touches I had ever felt, and I felt especially special because I had someone to play dolls with- a girl. And she embraced me in the calmest way possible and I felt I was hers and then she invited her younger brother one day to play as well and we became both of hers. Her karma came quick. She was raped, and when they told me I was sitting in a black computer chair, and I cried, um I cried. And I knew that I was shedding tears that belonged to me. I cried because it was owed to me, and I cried because I never wanted anyone to be a victim."

"At times, all we can do is sit back and listen, and my dear, this is one of those times. If you aren't too affected, we can move onto the other friends," she said.

"God places people into our lives for a reason; whether they are forever or seasonal is up to Him. Misty and Kiesha are consumed with this world, and our beliefs do not match. Misty is what this world calls 'conscious,' and Kiesha was raised in the church but is so honored to follow behind this world. We simply don't match. I don't speak how they speak or think how they do. They are the high of the society," I said.

"What's the high of the society, Janee?" Tara asked

"In one's eyes, the view may be blurry, complexity surrounding the pupil. The corner of the eye closed off, dreams and stress cloud the mind. Eventually melting and seeping into the eyes. Your eyes are impermeable and faded out, and that's the true high of society. You see, if anything can get through you, you're a part of this world. If you let the things of the world cloud your judgment, then you are the society," I said.

"That makes sense, I love how you use words to express yourself," Tara said.

"When it comes to friends or any relationship, I give my all. I have bought cars for people; I have given my last; I have been nothing but genuine. And people see that and feed off of it. My God father said I have a heart of gold, and this is great and truly a gift, but it is also dangerous-"

Tara interrupting said, "You must guard your heart because everything flows through it. That's scripture, girl!"

That was why we got along so well.

"Janee, I am going to give you an assignment," she began.

I crunched my face in desire and interest.

"I want you to elaborate on all of your relationships- down to the T. I want you to pull from inside yourself, expand on every relationship, and find the comparisons. I want a letter by our next meeting. Don't B.S it either; I know how thorough you can be," she finished.

I rolled my eyes and jumped up, "Let me find out you know my life," I said.

I decided to get this "assignment" out of the way as soon as I got home. I cracked out my phone and began typing. She was getting an email.

Expectations:

I find myself angered and even more so saddened. Saddened because I made up all these expectations in my head, you know the ones like, 'if they don't love me a certain way, then they don't at all.' I burst into tears about shit that hasn't even happened, shit that might happen, and shit that did happen, and shit that is happening. I feel the past, I feel the present, and at times my heart aches for the future. I have a heart, I feel. I feel all too much because of expectations. Really, I've built these expectations pretty much saying my way or the highway, over exaggerating my place in people's hearts and trying to make everything make sense. As soon as my expectations fail, I find myself angered, weary, and down and out, stuck in my own head, breaking my own heart once more. Pretty insane, right?

I constantly speak on how I can't stand being put into a box- lumped up into the same category as others. I get defensive and attempt to cause an uproar every time someone does it to me. Well, it seems I have been doing the same. There are rules in this world; there are ways to do things; however, just because someone doesn't choose the ways I choose doesn't make them right or wrong. It makes them, them. I'll give my last, and others will devote their time. Some will write thoughtful letters; others will send a simple daily text. My way isn't the only way to do things. There's more to this life besides Janee's world.

Friends:

Anger and sadness abruptly came onto my doorstep regarding friends. Every time I thought I had one, something went left. I'd give my all trying to show myself as a good friend, and most took my heart and ran with it. And not in a loving way. I found myself anxious for the old ones to come back. Just one moment like the ones we used to have, just one familiar memory to ease me. Buying their love while fighting for one of the top spots in their lives. They never came, we just didn't fit together. The relationship was gone, and I let them burn the bridge.

No one wants to be walked all over, but who says having a good heart means you're a doormat? Just because certain people go out their way beyond others means nothing. I am trying to initiate unconditional love: if I have, you have; if you need me, I'm there, and lastly, I forgive you always and forever. There is still nothing in this world that anyone can do to me that would cause me not to forgive them.

Christ is an excellent friend to me; it doesn't get any better than my father God- I'm just trying to be like my daddy. So, I will no longer depress myself about the people that strayed away from me, and when they come back, I'll be here. I will not stop my heart because it's who I am. I will love endlessly no matter how the odds may be against me and others. I want people to feel loved unconditionally; I'm rooting for love.

Now, as far as losing friends, I have learned that I was completely wrong in my teens. That loyalty was there, but my resistance to change made the loyalty pointless. See, as I was changing after so much resistance, I wanted my friends to change at that exact moment. While I was changing, I was also stuck in the past- if I wasn't going to sleep over every few weeks, or if we weren't going to hang out at the same spot, doing the same things then I didn't want the friendship at all. And I believed this because I couldn't think of any future that could be better than the past. I was so used to that insanity, it had become comforting, and I enjoyed it because it wasn't all bad. That's what happened between Kiesha, Misty, and me. As they went on to different paths, I couldn't understand why things didn't remain the same. I didn't understand how they could build bonds with other people and why they wanted to actively follow this world. I believed they had no conscious and that I was the only one struggling in my mind with all the wrongdoing I was partaking in. But see, perception is amazing because just as adamant as I was about my beliefs, they were about theirs. I didn't have to cut them off.

I didn't have to compare myself to them- I had the opportunity to actually prove that loyalty and realness that I regularly preached. But I passed up the opportunity and turned my back on an opportunity to practice what I preach. Why? Because of expectations and a lack of understanding. I finally realized even though I'd forgive someone, as quickly as they'd hurt me was as quickly as I'd throw them away. People had become disposable in my eyes.

Family:

I remember wishing that they'd let me sleep at other people's houses. Because the predators were in my house. It was a twisted hell, and I couldn't help but laugh. I recently found how grooming is related to sexual abuse. All this time, I thought I had lied because I had begun to like it. But that chaos was instilled, I was trained, and when I stopped resisting, they found their freedom from corruption. Now I was allowing myself. Now I was my worst enemy. So, forgive them, HA! I lied to myself as I glorified the importance of forgiveness, I pick and choose who I will forgive. I felt like if I forgave, I was betraying my healing, my future, my accomplishments, and my testimony. I felt none of it would be valid, and it wouldn't be real. Because if this really happened, how could I ever forgive them? So, I began to wonder if I am a predator, or am I a victim? I have been both, so while I'm forgiving myself, I will forgive all of them. My one time is the same as their many times because once they were victims. And I'm crazy enough to believe no one took the time to help them heal. So, I invite them all to heal through me and let day one of recovery and repentance occur. As I said before, none are one hundred percent good or bad. We have all been a hero and a villain.

How was that?

See you soon,
Janee.

Tara never responded, but I got the point quickly. I needed the release.

Chapter Eleven

ONE FLESH

"Where ya off to, girly?" Annie asked before I could touch the door.

"To the movies, Mom," I answered.

"With T?"

"But of course," I answered with a smile.

"I'm so happy you found a good friend. Have fun, sweetie."

"Will do."

"So, would you say, your loved ones approved of you and T's friendship?"

"For the most part, yes."

"And exactly what does that mean?"

"Everyone accepted it until they started really paying attention."

"I need examples. Please don't hold back."

"Hey, Charlie."

"Hi, love."

"Come here a second I have to talk to you about something."

"Is it about that girl, O'Shai?"

"Girl, who? You mean Tasha?

"Yeah, that one that likes you."

"She definitely doesn't like me. That's just my best friend."

"Mhm. I don't know anyone who sits and talks to someone on the phone for hours, wakes up, and falls asleep on the phone with them, and also spends all their time with them. THE GIRL LIKES YOU."

"No. I'm not her type. She likes those gorgeous girls that society loves and that look, act, and dress like each other. Besides, she said she thinks you and Sapphire are cute, of course."

"Girl, she still likes you."

I ain't falling for that bullshit, I thought. Hope in something that will never be.

"Well, she said she would like to talk to you. And if you guys do, I'll be okay with that."

"I'm not going to do that to you because I know you like her. Besides, what am I going to do with that little girl?" she chuckled.

"Oh. So, we've gotten down to the real story. Tell me more about these feelings. Did they progress? Fade away? Or what?"

The phone rang.

"Hey, Best Friend! You know you are one of the only people that can brighten up my day. I love you, Best Friend."

"Hey T. Aw, how cute," I blushed.

"So, did you talk to Charlie?"

"Yes, I just finished talking to her about fifteen minutes ago."

"So, what did she say? I could just imagine the smirk on her face."

"Well, I told her. And she said that she isn't really interested," I said, trying to end the conversation.

"Why not?" she chased.

"Well…" I answered right before my voice started to shake. "She said she wouldn't do that to me."

"Wait, huh? What does that mean, Best Friend?"

"Oh, nothing. What are you doing?" I responded, trying to change the subject.

"Yes, it is. Tell me."

"Well, she said that since I like you that I should tell you. But, I told her I know I'm not your type, so you guys should try things out."

"What is my type, Janee?" she asked with a tiny laugh.

The phone clicked.

"Why did you hang up the phone? You were really doing well with expressing your feelings to her. So, what made you hang up?"

"I just felt that there was no point. She knows what she likes, and I just don't fit that description."

"The image that society portrays on how women should look?"

"Yes. That one."

"How did you know she wasn't willing to try something different?"

"I never said this story was over, Tara."

All the things that had gone through my head that year seemed to gang up on me that night. My thoughts tormented me, and as I tried to fight it, I grew weaker. Being free from self-harm for a year meant nothing at that moment. I never wanted so badly to press a gun to my head. That's how it feels with all the pressure. You've been nothing but a trigger. So, familiar, lovely, and dark. Ah, sanity.

There was a knock at the door.

I paused my music.

"Janee!" one of my other roommates, Melinda, yelled outside my door. "Janee, let me in."

"It's unlocked," I grumbled

"Now, what the fuck is wrong with you? All I can hear is Tell Me Lies by Ann Marie, from your door. And that's a shame because you had on headphones," she chastised.

"Nothing is wrong. I just like the song," I lied.

"Now bitch, you know something is wrong because I surely do," she said, still pushing.

"How do you figure that, Mel?" I asked while still trying to play my role.

"BECAUSE YOUR ROOM IS A DAMN MESS," she yelled. "And I talked to T. She said she keeps calling and texting you, but you won't answer. What is going on?"

"I'm just not feeling it," I murmured.

"May I ask-"

"Now, Tara, you know you're going to ask, so why ask about asking?" I interrupted.

"Exactly. Why wouldn't you answer her calls and texts? She was reaching out to you."

"She doesn't care."

"It seems so. Why do you think she doesn't care?"

"Because she never has."

"Explain."

"Did I ever tell you the story when I was infamous on YouTube at the end of tenth grade?"

"No. But you always did say people harassed you in high school."

"It was more than that."

"Care to share now?"

"The second trimester in tenth grade was the time I did a complete 180. I got straight A's for the first time when I got suspended for two weeks-"

"I don't mean to cut you off, but was that the time after you punched your classmate Ashley in the face after you guys got off the school bus?"

"Ding, ding."

"Okay. Keep going."

"Well, that was also the year I dropped forty pounds, and I got a bunch of attention."

"Yes, you expressed that you didn't like it because it wasn't genuine."

"Exactly. Well, about two weeks before school ended for the summer, I got into it with this upperclassman named DeShawn after school. I rejected a sexual gesture earlier that year, and I assumed he was salty about that. Anyways, one thing led to another, and he pushed me down. I got up as quick as ever and popped him dead straight in his face. The whole time T and DeShawn's friend Michael were recording, but the thing is T was in front of Michael's camera when I jumped up, and molly whopped DeShawn's face. So, long story short, Michael and DeShawn uploaded it to YouTube and named it DeShawn and The Fat Bitch Fight."

"Wow. That had to be humiliating."

"Yes, I never heard the last of it. People spoke about it and talked about me for years. Even after DeShawn sincerely apologized the following year."

"I'm glad he apologized. What does this have to do with Tasha?"

"She didn't defend me. Ever since I met her, I defended her. There were several times when I got in trouble for defending her. People throwing shit at her, talking about her, calling her names, and so on. Tasha has never defended me. She will say how something is fucked up before or after the fact. But she would and has never defended me. The truth is she hasn't cared enough to."

"I completely understand. That would upset me as well. Would you say that caused a strain on your friendship? What made her not defend you on that day?"

"Her excuse was that we weren't close. But it's funny because I remember hanging out with her. I remember laughing with her."

"Excuse my language, Janee, but that's truly fucked up."

"T, earth to T," I yelled.

"Yeah. Sorry, Best Friend, I'm texting the baby bottle pop," she joked.

"Don't come for my daughter, T."

"YOU ARE THE ONE WHO NAMED HER THAT."

"That's because she's young and ditsy. Just like all the girls you've talked to and only talked to," I shaded.

"Oh, shut up. What about you and Travis?"

"Oh bitch, no you don't! That was one time. This is a reoccurring thing for you."

"One time was enough. You fell hard for that nigga."

"You right," I smirked. "So, what are y'all talking about?"

"She wants me to come see her since you and I are leaving River Days. But I told her I'm not going unless you come 'cause you ma best friend. Go best friend," she began to sing.

"T, you are going to drive all the way to Jackson, Michigan?"

"Only if you come. It's an hour or so drive."

"I'm down. Just take me back to the building really quick, so I can change into my comfy clothes. And turn up the air; it's hot as fuck."

"Yasss, bitch, yaaaas."

"Okay, so you are okay with meeting a girl that T has been talking to? Does this mean you no longer have feelings for her?"

"I'm trying to be a supportive friend. Just because I like her, and it may seem that she likes me, but doesn't mean we are necessarily meant to be."

"That's mature of you. And I'm glad you care about her enough to let her go."

"I tried to let her go. I tried."

"Shall, we cue the-"

"Dun, dun, dun," we teased in unison.

"Look, T," I said while pointing at a girl. "That's the eleventh girl I've seen today that is your type," I teased seriously.

"What type, Best Friend? You always say that shit."

"You know, T."

"And what's your so-called 'type' Best Friend?"

"It used to be Middle Eastern guys. Or really just guys surrounded by culture. Foreign, I guess."

"So, what's wrong with what I like? Seems like you like the same."

"Each guy I dated was different for the most part. Some were bad boys, others mama's boys, highly intelligent ones, business-orientated ones, and most a mix of all these qualities."

"I'm not getting what you're trying to say, Best Friend."

"What I'm trying to say is, I was and am always willing to date someone who is nice to me. Someone who looks out for me. Yes, someone with goals and ambition, but I don't have many requirements for that. I will always give someone a chance who seems to have my best interests at heart."

"Okay, what makes that different from the girls I like? They all had or still have feelings for me."

"It just seems like you date to impress others. You give only certain girls a chance if you know people will be jealous or just so you can be like, 'yeah, I can pull this'."

"It just takes a lot to get my attention."

"But, they have gotten your attention, and they have almost all ended up being the exact same or similar. I guess I just really don't understand why you couldn't give me a chance. I don't get what you think is wrong with me."

"Best Friend, it really isn't you. No one has had my attention. Not even, Kyla, or as you call her, Baby Bottle Pop." She laughed. "I'm just trying to get my shit together. I don't want to talk to or be in a relationship with anyone."

"I can respect that, T."

"Did Tasha telling you that she is focusing on herself make you feel any better?"

"Yes, it did for a short time."

"Why a short time?"

"The attachment started getting too comfortable."

"Best Friend, give me a kiss," T urged while I resisted.

"Nah, hoe. I don't know where those lesbian lips have been."

"Best Friend, you're not getting out my car until you give me my kiss."

"Okay fine," I said as I kissed her on her cheek. "EW! You freak." I jokingly pulled away before she could kiss my mouth.

"No, you are my best friend. I can get me a kiss from my best friend," she teased.

"Get away from me, duck," I burst out laughing.

"That's not fair; I let you give me birthday kisses."

"Girl, you didn't even let me finish."

"Yes, I did."

"No. Let me finish," I blushed. "One, mwah, two, mwah, three, mwah, four, mwah," I continued kissing her until, "eighteen, mwah, ANDDDDD NINETEEN, mwah."

"Aw, Best Friend, now it's my turn."

"No, it's not my birthday!" I teased. "FaceTime me A.S.A.P, hoe," I demanded while getting out the car.

"Alright, Best Friend," she responded after slapping my butt. "Oooooo yaaas, that ass."

"You disgust me," I screamed.

"Now, when did all this flirting start?"

"Surprising, shortly after I told her my feelings."

"Did it ever subside?"

"Hell no, Tara, hell no."

"Dukes, did you watch the video?"

"Yes, it was whack. She didn't know what she was doing."

"You talking all shit but haven't sent me anything better." Was she really challenging me right now?

"Yeah, whatever, it's sending now."

"See. I knew you were a freak."

"Bitch, please! I'm innocent."

"Best Friend, let me see."

"See what?"

"Let me seeeee."

"See these nuts, hoe."

"Janee! Can I come in?" Mel screamed from outside my door.

"Girl, I don't care."

"What are you doing?" she asked while glancing at the phone, "HEY SEXY ASS T," she screamed.

"What's good?" T responded.

"Man, if y'all don't get y'all lesbianism away from me," I joked.

"That's so funny seeing that you and T are in love and whatnot." Her and her smart-ass mouth.

"Girl byeeee," I refuted.

"Anyways, I was just looking at all these dicks."

"Ain't God good. SHE'S DELIVERED!" I said while raising my hands high, laughing, but very serious.

"Girl, bye," she said as she flicked me off with T laughing in the background. "I'm talking about strap-ons."

Handing me the phone to view the picture, "Why is that one so big?" I responded.

"We all know it's not what you're used to," T laughs.

"Shut up, but that is true."

"Aw, Best Friend, do you want me to use a strap on you?"

I ignored her while browsing more pictures with Mel.

"Best Friend?" she repeated.

"Bitch, answer her," Mel demanded me.

"Yes?" I asked, trying to act annoyed and oblivious.

"I said, do you want me to use a strap on you?"

Is she serious?! What type of games?! Just chaos and foolishness, I thought.

"Hmmmmm," Tara said, looking as if she was contemplating. "I can definitely see your frustration with this."

"We began doing what I consider love taps. Which is basically feeling on each other quickly and or pinching each other," I paused in frustration. "It was all so confusing. I kept getting crushed because I didn't know why she wouldn't choose me. Was I not popular enough, pretty enough, too fat?" Tara frowned. "I began feeling so worthless, but so content being around her. I didn't know if I wanted to cuss her out, kiss her, or block her. And as my frustration grew, my loved ones began to notice."

"Yaaaaas. Church was good today! CHECK ME, LORD," I proclaimed while laughing with other members.

"I feel much better," T said as she grabbed her phone off the chair.

"Janee," Daniel called.

"Yes, Dad?

"Come in here. I want to talk to you."

We walked into the office, and he shut the door with his head tilted upward as if he were thinking hard about something.

"Does that girl like you, Nae?"

"No. I don't think so." I knew they'd figure it out.

"Okay, Nae. But you have to be careful. You can't let anything taint your anointing, you've come too far," he urged.

"I know."

Oh, and boy did I know. Everything she did or said, or I did, was about her, and it bothered me in both the most satisfying and torturous ways possible.

"How did T like church the other day?" Annie asked as I was coming down the steps. "I did overhear her saying she felt better."

"She said she really liked it," I responded. "Did you see those tears?"

"Awwww, yes! She broke down as soon as I began praying for her."

I smiled, then paused.

"Sit down and talk to me, Nae."

I sat.

"You said there was a time when you liked girls." I nodded. "Well, is that stuff coming back up?"

"Yes," I responded while nodding.

"Okay. Did it start coming back up when you started hanging out with T?"

I began to cry.

"Does she like you too? I knew I could feel something between you too."

"Mhm," I said while wiping my nose. "I just don't get what's wrong with me. She acts like she likes me but then looks at or gives attention to something completely different."

"But is that even something you really want? To be in a relationship with another girl?" I shrugged my shoulders. "It's time for you to pull out your war scriptures. You have to fight this."

"I know."

"Even if you two were to be together, it wouldn't work out. You guys are on two totally different paths." I looked up at her. "You are a faithful church member. You want the best for your life, and the best for you is with Christ included fully. It won't work. Remember what the Bible says about being evenly yoked?" I nodded. "Without being evenly yoked, you two cannot possibly be one flesh."

"How did you feel about Annie giving you that advice?" Tara asked with concern.

"I appreciated the fact that she could recognize I was going through something. I loved her advice, but I have always been so hardheaded."

"Did you pick the seats yet?" T asked.

"This takes time, hoe. You know I'm not tech-savvy." I continued searching. "Got it. Finding Dory starts at 2:30 p.m."

"I'm on my way."

"You are hardheaded," Tara said while shaking her head.

I said sarcastically, giving T the death stare, "So, you're going to be on your phone the whole time?" She kept texting. "JUST LIKE YOU WERE THE WHOLE FUCKING MOVIE."

"Chill," she responded, still texting.

"You are so fucking rude."

"Ok."

"Is this the first time T ignored you like this? She definitely seemed uninterested on this particular day."

"Let me just explain to you how Tasha is. Tasha doesn't give a fuck. That can be a very good thing as well as a very bad thing." I paused.

"So, you're saying this is common for her?"

"Once we started talking all the time and she knew I liked her, I felt like she started taking advantage of it."

"How so?"

"She would do shit like this, be on her phone the whole time we hung out or as I felt, purposely called other girls cute or showed me their pictures. It felt like torture. I'd try to explain how I felt. Text her paragraphs, and she'd only read the first and last sentence and respond to the last. Whenever we talked on the phone, she'd change the subject or cover it up by saying, 'I love you, Best Friend'. As soon as I'd be cool with us being friends and possibly as well as most likely not being her type or what she would ever want, she'd start flirting again." I paused again, looking down at the floor. "I just snapped. Right in front of her and I needed help right then and right there."

"Hey, Nae," my aunt Candance said after picking up the phone.

"Hi, Auntie," I said, trying to fight my tears.

"What's wrong, sweetie?"

I already knew she knew what was wrong. She always knew- Her and mom.

"I can't take it anymore. I can't deal with a person that never thinks I'm good enough but wants to string me along. I'm so tired of it," I said through pauses and sniffles.

T looked at me for a moment and then started her car up, beginning to drive.

"Nae, I was waiting for you to come and talk to me about this, you already know that."

Sniffing, I replied, "You couldn't just call me or sent me a text? You knew. You always know."

"You think because I'm blessed to have God give me this gift that I would just move without him saying so?"

"No, ma'am."

"Okay then. Where is she, Nae?"

"Right here."

T glanced at me while driving.

Sighing, she replied, "Nae, you have to separate yourself from her. And you have to be careful with this because you can't taint her walk with Christ. You may just as well be that light that brings her to him. He could very well be using you."

"Okay, I will," I said, wiping my tears.

"Okay sweetie, call me when you get home."

"I wonder how Tasha felt seeing you break down like that." I began looking at the floor again. "I can't imagine that she didn't notice, and I don't think she didn't care."

"I know," I murmured.

"So, what happened?"

"Well, I told her that we needed to separate and that I was sorry. I told her it sounds so fucked up because I had to separate from her because of her liking girls and the fact that it was affecting me. It hurt me so much to tell her this because it would kill me if someone had to separate from me because of what I like." Tara listened intently. "But of course, faithful old Tasha understood. Tasha always understands."

Two months later.

"What's wrong, Janee?" Mel asked while storming into my room.

"I'm tired of Tasha's shit."

Rolling her eyes, "Oh God, what happened now?"

"I unblocked her because I was bored and I miss her, of course," Mel stared, "And I FaceTime'd her-"

"Yeah, let it ring once, then she called back like always, right?" she interrupted.

"Right," I said, smiling. "It's just so different now."

"I'm really tired of you crying over her. Annie was right. She takes advantage of your kindness, Janee."

I stared at the floor.

She continued. "She knows you'll always be there for her."

I took a deep breath. "That closure that she decided to give me was just a lot." Mel shook her head. "To find out she had been lying to me all summer."

"But you already knew that, Janee. I saw first-hand how she played with your feelings. And if you were her best friend, how could she lie to you constantly all these months?"

Staring at the floor, "I always looked out for her, but it's time for her to grow up. I can't be there for her. It's time for me to start slowly pulling away."

"It really is, Janee. Come on, girl. We definitely can't miss church today," Mel said, pulling me off my bed.

We entered the church as Daniel was in the middle of preaching. "God made a promise to us," he paused, "but the promise he made was for salvation. He didn't say when he would bless us or how. That is not what the promise is. This is the reason we cannot exchange God for something else," he paused again. "We may not want to give up a certain thing, but God is saying that we can't have that bad habit and him. He is urging us to drop that very thing that is getting in the way of being blessed and getting closer to him. If we choose to keep playing with God, we will get what we want but lose what we had. Don't let God have to take his hands off of you to let go of that very thing that you desire. He is warning and trying to prevent you from much heartache, and it's not as desirable as you think."

I felt attacked. Check me, Lord.

I began praying. Lord, I know you are speaking to me, and I am finally ready to listen. Lord, please do not take your hands off of me. Please forgive me. All I ask is how to let this go? Please help me to let this situation go. I choose you, Lord. I surrender!

Chapter Twelve

HOLDING YOU CLOSE TO MY HEART

"Hi sweetie, how's your studying going?" Annie asked.

"It's going great, Mom; I'm just reflecting on what Dad preached yesterday. We really do have to make sacrifices to see the marvelous works of God. I'm deciding what sacrifices I need to make," I said. "It is also important that when we make these sacrifices, they are just that, a sacrifice. If we are simply giving up sweets, and we don't care for sweets, then that isn't a true sacrifice."

"That's awesome; you realize how imperative it is to study God's word and follow him throughout your life. The sacrifices will come, and your obedience will bring on great rewards from God," she said.

"I know, I'm ready to make the step. I've sacrificed celibacy; now, I really need to work on my mouth. I'm sure Makayla can help. She can bleep out all the profanity in any song," I said, chuckling.

Mom smiled, shaking her head, "Yeah, that's my child. We just have to work on Mil now," she said.

"Oh God," I laughed. "Give me fifteen more minutes, and we can get going on our outing!"

"Take your time. We have plenty of time to celebrate our sixth anniversary; it isn't even 4:31 yet!" she joked. I entered Victory House on April 22, 2013 at 4:31pm.

That dedication to the Lord brought nothing but glory to my life. I was building and maintaining relationships, and I felt like I was enough. And this time, I hadn't given the credit to my new best friend 200mg of Lamictal. Sometimes you need just some little milligrams and a whole lot of Jesus! That was all God's doing. When I praised God or learned about Him, I found sanity. I felt safe. And as crazy as it sounds, being safe scared me.

Annie

My angel, my angel. I can't thank Annie enough for stepping into my life and sticking. I have never met a woman so admirable and giving. I resisted her. I resisted her so much. I didn't understand her peace, her grace, or her love. I didn't feel worthy, so I resisted, but she never left. She never left me, and I can never thank God enough for the mother he has blessed me with. I often speak about the bad because it's comforting; because I find myself crying more when I think of the good. But I can't thank God enough for a human that I have cried about so much because of how much of a blessing they are.

Quintessential

"Janee," Mom called. "Do you know who Vashti is in the Bible?" she asked.

"I recall her pertaining to the story of Esther," I said.

"Yes, but she played a major role as one of the many women in the Bible, despite her reputation," she said. "Vashti is considered a woman of modesty. She was an absolutely beautiful woman. So beautiful, her husband, Persian King Ahasuerus, also known as Xerxes, assumed it was appropriate to display her beauty at a feast whose company was all but upright. Queen Vashti was aware of the importance of obeying her husband and the fact that he was King. However, she also was certain that only her husband was to gaze upon her, not drunk men at a feast with concubines. Vashti upheld modesty and self-worth. She honored her life and knew what she brought to the table; she was the prize. She was also confident that she had every right to refuse because God made it clear that her beauty was between her and her husband, solely. She demanded respect."

"I've never viewed Vashti's deposition in that way. Others perceive her as humiliating the King and disobedient. This changes my view of the story," I said "Janee, that's who you are! You are the prize; everyone can't have access to you. Vashti is imperative. She taught women and even men the importance of saying, 'NO.' No, to value self-worth and preserve integrity. I need you to build up your 'no,' Janee."

"I understand," I said.

"Do you baby?" she asked. "No, you can't call me out my name. No, I won't and don't have to buy your love. No, you can't drop me off at work while you drive my car. No, I won't let you treat me anyway. No, I won't be treated like a doormat. NO, I WON'T BUY YOU THAT BELT," she said.

We both laughed.

"We are laughing, but I'm serious. Janee, you have to build up your 'no'. If they don't treat you like a queen- and that pertains to friendships, relationships, family ties, jobs, etc.—if they don't treat you like the queen YOU ARE, tell them BYE. Recognize, love, and cling to your self-worth, woman of God. A 'woman of power', a 'queen'. You accept and love the beauty and assignment God has given you. Build up your NO," she said.

Ahhh, one of many of Annie's great lessons. A pep talk without getting punched in my chest. Haha, I love her.

Daniel

I am listening. That's what I have to say about Daniel. I am here, and I am listening. I had never respected any man before I met Daniel. I resisted men and cringed, especially black men. Black men had treated me the worst, and I hated them for it. Until I soul searched and realized they were treating me the way I viewed myself.

Daniel never violated me. He never groomed me for anything but healing and growth in God. He's the only man I wouldn't mind falling asleep around, the only man that I would trust with my truth and the only man I will call Dad.

"Dad, what is an admonisher?" I asked after walking into his study.

"An admonisher can be looked at as someone who warns, a reminder, someone who cares for others. So, in a sense, a guardian," he said. "Why do you ask, sweetie?"

"Elder told me something at church last week while he was praying for me. He said I am a praiser, a worshiper, a joy giver, and an admonisher. He urged me to increase the joy I give and pull people to worship God. He said that would be my deliverance," I said.

"Oh. I see," he said, thinking.

"Was Jeremiah an admonisher?" I asked.

"Well, Janee, Jeremiah did warn people of their wrongdoings and need of repentance. I can see the connection," he said. "What made you reference Jeremiah?"

"Mom asked us in bible expository to touch on who we identify with in the Bible the most," I answered.

"And who did you come up with?" he asked.

"Well, I tinkered with this, Dad. I didn't know if I related to Isaiah- a poet who told about the hope for peace and righteousness on earth. Maybe Elijah because he feared no man and was a great impression on people's minds; Paul, because he was a remarkable writer and handled many things for God through writing. I learned to reach many people through writing, and I am bold as he was. But Jeremiah stuck with me, with the help of Brother Luke. Jeremiah was constantly persecuted for obeying God, even when he did not want to. Jeremiah was chosen by God, for correction, and he was beaten for it. It seems I'm always bold (in God), always trying to teach what I know about the word and how it has improved me, but I am commonly tormented for doing so," I said.

"Janee, Jeremiah is the book of prophecy. Sometimes God calls us during moments that are trying. Because I know you struggle with your peers disliking you and are earnestly trying to edify God by following him, although you know only pieces of the plans He has for you, I will allow you to read next week's message," he said. "Here. Use it to build your confidence in your future as well. And I think it may also further identify your connection with Jeremiah."

Daniel handed me his handwritten notes which said this:

Jeremiah: the book of prophecy
The call of Jeremiah

> Jeremiah 1:1-5, "The words of Jeremiah the son of Hilkiah, of the priests that were in Anathoth in the land of Benjamin: to whom the word of the Lord came in the days of Josiah the son of Amon king of Judah, in the thirteenth year of his reign. It came also in the days of Jehoiakim the son of Josiah king of Judah, unto the end of the eleventh year of Zedekiah the son of Josiah king of Judah, unto the carrying away of Jerusalem captive in the fifth month. Then the word of the Lord came unto me, saying, Before I formed thee in the belly I knew thee; and before thou camest forth out of the womb I sanctified thee, and I ordained thee a prophet unto the nations."
>
> Jeremiah 29:11, "For I know the thoughts that I think toward you, saith the Lord, thoughts of peace, and not of evil, to give you an expected end." No one can change your direction or path except you and not receive this greatness from God. You can testify to the world, you're great! This is a plan God has already established- the only thing you can be prideful about.

The calling of Jeremiah happened in a time where things were chaotic. Not every time when God calls us is in a good moment. Sometimes when you are called, you are called to ministry during rough times. God needs a body of people to stand firm in spite of opposition: He needs a vessel. Will you and are you ready to live up to the standard of God's calling?

A faithful person of God, Jeremiah stands in attention at God's command, ready to move as instructed. And the person doesn't care whose feelings get hurt because there is a purpose. A rebuke is to get people back in order. God used Jeremiah to prophet and rebuke so the people could come back to Him to be blessed. Sometimes there is a standard you must live by to be great and set an example for others to be blessed.

Destined doesn't mean you are going to be great. It's a plan, and you choose your path. God wants it for you, but do you want it? God will not share His glory with any other. How dare you set your standards to a period where God can't bless you! God wants us to live in the overflow- when we can proudly say, it's raining on me!

God deals with us in stages of development. Nothing happens without order; God does nothing without order. God is using those uncomfortable moments to establish Himself, to get your attention. Your bad news and unpleasant moments are your opportunities for God to establish. You can't understand experience with no conflict. Experience is the best teacher! God wants to make you great, so I have to speak out for the house to flow right.

You have to wait your turn. You have to watch other people winning while you are uncomfortable. You have to wait on God to bless you to build that experience. What do we do when God interrupts our plans? Those who feel as though they are mess-ups, God wants to use you as a come-up. God has to pull certain things out of people, for you to be great because not everyone wants to be blessed. God says to Jeremiah, 'do not say you are inexperienced, stop making excuses, stop believing it can't be done for you.' Stop saying God can't use you because of what has happened and is happening. Your mess-ups don't change God's plans.

Jeremiah lacked self-confidence. The word of the Lord came to him. God touched Jeremiah's mouth, and the touch triggered the anointing. There was a plan, a purpose, and then came an anointing. Lord, touch me! Make me great in You! Allow God to touch you if you want to be great."

"I see the correlation," I said soon after.

If anyone asked me what makes me happy or what my happiness is, I would present Daniel and Annie, my angels. I can't talk much about happiness because it is something you feel and have to see before your eyes. I am not gifted to write my happiness, only my pain, and or deep thoughts. But I'd love to show anyone my happiness; I'd love to show anyone my parents.

A few hours later.

"Janee, you are so happy today! You are glowing," Tara said, welcoming me into her office.

"I'm so happy," I began to weep. "I was just telling the congregation yesterday at bible study how happy I am."

"I am elated that you have such a remarkable church family. I truly enjoyed myself last Sunday when I visited!" she said.

"Don't be misled. Everything isn't perfect, but overall, I am happy," I said.

"Well, let's look into the things and situations that are lacking in your life," she said. "I know you have dedicated much of your time to gaining that close relationship with God, and as filling out worksheets I have given you for strengthening and maintaining relationships. What else is bothering you?"

"Girl, men," I started. "It seems like none of them want me. I had one guy ask me why I was even looking when my life seems so perfect; he told me I was intimidating."

"Well, I hope you would recognize that those men are what your sister Makayla calls trash," she chuckled.

"Haha, I do, but I still get lonely," I said.

"Do not get discouraged- God has the perfect man that will compliment you in every way," she promised.

"I know. It's just hard to wait."

"Oh, that celibacy is getting difficult for you?" she said as I smiled. "Hang in there. It will all be worth it. Two years is a long time- you must feel some type of fulfillment."

"Yes, but year two is kicking my butt."

That was because I was certain that I am a girl who has not been found, I have no name- no one's around. But somehow, my past consumed it all, and somehow, I'm someone who belongs to all.

When I was twenty-something.

Monday, November 20, 2017, at 7:49 a.m., a text from Daniel read:

"Good morning. I am not going to call you Janee. I am going to address you as 'Woman of God. Last night I dreamed a dream. In this dream, I saw you and Annie sitting down, and you started singing songs of worship. Then Annie joined in. As you were doing so, I saw the number 150 falling over you. Here comes the break down from the spiritual side.

In theology there is God, then there are angels. From this point, a coded message is being given that no one has access to but you. The coded message 150 is broken down to the one, five, and the zero. The five is very powerful. Five is grace, and also in the natural realm of angels. It means to not put yourself in the position to be a pushover. Meaning, do not belittle yourself for the sake of relationships that you want to work. In this season, you have to stand up for yourself. The one is new beginning. There are projects and opportunities, but these doors just won't open...they can be opened by your thoughts, beliefs, and actions. The zero represents the outcome and beginning of a spiritual journey. In this thought, the Bible says, 'Lean not on your own understanding. Acknowledge Him, and He shall direct your path.' If you allow that to be the objective of your journey, then your journey will be blessed- the coded message 150 means to put in that extra effort. Do not be frustrated by distractions. Be positive in spite of your challenges. God bless.... love you much."

Two months later, I found myself barging into Tara's door two minutes before our session was due to start.

Part 2: Giving up My All

After fulfilling two years, eight months, and two weeks of celibacy, I broke. I broke because I was vulnerable, and I broke because, why not? I had a dream I associated with the wrong people, and I dwelled in my desires. I wasn't forced, begged, or misled- I simply broke.

After spending about an hour and a half looking for a God-given sign on how to move forward, I decided to write my own opinion and plan. My hopes were up when I found a blog entitled, "I had sex after two years of celibacy," at the end, the gentleman quoted Pony by Genuine, "If you're horny, let's do it." After more searching, I found three others that started off relatable then turned into bible bashing. I loathe that. To say the least, I couldn't find ANYTHING.

"And what did you write, love?" she asked.

"I have to first explain the ride to his house: The thought, "don't go," shook my whole body. I said a prayer and ignored it. The first time I had ever been sure it was God, I heard him loud and clear."

"Continue," she said.

I grabbed my iPhone and began reading:

"Four years and eight months ago, I met a man through an online dating site. He was a delightful young man: smart, kind- he was doing what he was supposed to do and was what he was supposed to be. It didn't take us long to connect as friends, and then eventually, after two years, the confusion sprouted. 'That will be your husband,' 'he sounds jealous,' 'well, you left him in Novi. I'd say he likes you and he's a bit crazy,' 'the way he looks at you.' Words from people looking from the outside in. This young man never declared his love, but actions told otherwise.

"Nevertheless, I was comfortable around him, and he made me feel safe. He wasn't mine, and I wasn't his, we weren't married, let alone even together. Being in a relationship with each other had never come up in any conversation of ours.

"How was it? A long two years and my vagina completely rejected him. He still didn't force it; he was still kind. He cuddled with me for an hour after and made me laugh as soon as I was brave enough to show my wet face and red squinty eyes.

"My ride home: I felt nothing.

"Day two: I felt everything. I prayed for God's forgiveness and for him to block any soul ties that were developing or preparing to do so. I wept, I wept, I wept. I pleaded, I shouted, and I worshipped. I wept again. What now Lord? After being so sure and committing myself to Him, what now? After hearing Him say 'don't go', what now? I had fallen short into a situationship. After all those years of harvesting, 2018 was the beginning of my winning season, and I broke. There is nothing I deserved prior to this and definitely nothing I deserve after this. What now, Lord? Do I start over and try again? This time aim for greater, cut anything sexual out fully? Cold turkey or baby steps?

"Here's where that lack of gray kicks in. I used to think everything was either black or white, either it is, or it isn't- no in-between no grays. Well in this situation, it will be just that. Glory be to God for his unconditional and undying love- I am the one beating myself up with guilt.

"Day four: actually, day one of my celibacy.

1. I will enjoy my singleness
2. I will commit myself to God, by seeking Him in everything I do
3. I will allow Him to work on me
4. I will surround myself with likeminded people
5. I will learn to be a wife (I guess I have to learn how to cook)
6. I will start over, and I will finish strong this time
7. Anything or anyone that needs to be cut will be cut. It is time for me to become my best friend rather than my worst enemy
8. The bad habits end now

9. Time to grow
10. Those bad seeds planted will never prevail

"It is still my winning season."

"wow, it sounds like you have done all your thinking and made up your mind as to what to do next. Why are you still in a fuss? We all fall short; the bible says even a just man falls short," she said.

"Because, Tara, three days later, I did it again, two weeks after that, again, and four days after that again," I cried. "And then the last time he told me he found another girl. She's an evangelist, and here I am throwing my values away for him, and he found someone like the old me."

"The old you? Honey, what does that mean?"

"I had a close relationship with God; He was and still is my everything. I was stronger back then. Now, look at me. I'm walking around confused with inner problems."

"Oh yeah, those soul ties are something else," she said.

"He completely did a 180. He attends church, he's in the word, and he's reading and writing. He's building that relationship. And all that is great, but I planted that seed. Why not with me?

It was a hell of a soul tie. One night after sex, we switched roles. I was speaking like him, and he was speaking like me before I had given up my celibacy. He went onward about God and the blessings that he wished to fill his life. Before he started all that, he looked at me and told me he had met someone else. He had pointed out that she was an evangelist and how she prayed for him. I felt my tears fill with the betrayal. All the time I had invested in that man, the sacrifices I had made. He broke through barriers that, for two years and eight months, no man could come close to breaking. I loved him with all my heart, not because of the attraction but because he was my friend. So, for him to look me in my eyes and betray me broke me," I said.

"It sounds like you soul swapped, he is you, and you are him. But you are original, and you will be able to become you once more and stronger. So, fall nine times and get back up ten, it's still your winning season. But how did he betray you? I know you mentioned all that you poured into him and the sacrifices, but what really was able to throw you over the edge?" Tara asked.

"The fact that he chose to be a man over our friendship. He chose to hurt me to satisfy himself. But what hurts the most was that he made it seem as if he didn't know what he was doing. Like I was ignorant or something," I said.

"What has helped you get over this? How was this such a huge lesson for you, like you pointed out in your email last week?" she asked.

"I saw how God could and had gotten the glory. He began reading the Bible more, his conversation changed, and his heart wanted so badly to change as well. It was truly like we were each other. He spoke the way I spoke, and he understood things. But I, I was lost, I was confused, and I was anxious. The hurt overwhelmed me, and everyone around me could see it. I chased that man every chance I could; I chased him in my mind, in my dreams, and anywhere else I could make him appear. Until one day, my Godfather, Daniel sat me down and revealed that the Lord had told him that I was falling. That this man was in my way, so much in my way that I was currently dying spiritually. And so, I was eager to pray for him, and I did it consistently until it healed me. I wished well over his life and hoped for good to surround him. I prayed for that man, not for him to love me, not for God to bring us together but for his soul. Because that's how much I loved him. That's how much I was determined to rebuke this spirit of heartache and confusion. I moved him out the way by unlatching that pain that connected me to him."

"That sounds amazing, Janee," Tara said.

"I also spoke to my godsister Makayla about this, and she gave me great advice about how he was very much a distraction and how distractions disrupt God's plan for us," I said.

"Care to go more in-depth?" Tara asked.

"She told me to look up the story of Samson in the Bible. Starting at Judges, the 13th chapter, which breaks down Samson, but mainly focusing on Judges 16: Samson and Delilah. She developed this message laid out like this:

Samson was thoughtful, well planned, and intentional. He had strength from his hair, which was a calling from God. Makayla tied that into God has placed strength, passion, etc. into us. But several things can become a distraction like friends, desires, and love. Distractions are a threat. Threats can destroy plans or purpose-for example, Delilah and Philistines.

Distractions can also remove the security of the plan or purpose; take out people, good and bad. If someone can distract you and get you until you're weak, the first thing they will do is take your vision, remove you to a new environment, so you won't know your surroundings, they will bind you with what can be bills, relationships, and even soul ties. They will humiliate you by asking where was your God?

But just one touch is all it takes. All it takes is a prayer and one touch from God. Even when we find ourselves distracted, God's plan will come to pass at any cost, but don't let it be at your expense. We can miss out on a lot by getting distracted; we want to be fruitful by accomplishing our purpose. There is a fine line between something being a distraction and a blessing. Resting and getting time with God, distractions don't happen immediately-it's a slow process. After so many distractions, you give in. But He will honor those sacrifices, those distractions that we turn away from. There is no peace outside of His territory.

Revelations 3:20 encourages us to make room for God. Judges 16:28 urges us to repent and ask for restoration. "I won't be held back, Tara, and I'm not defeated. The distraction happened, but like Makayla said, it only takes one touch from God, and I anticipate that touch every day," I finished.

"Well, you have certainly given me something to ponder on," she said.

Part 3: XoXoXo

Four months later

Subject: AIIIIIINNNNNNNNNNN! Too bad that resilience didn't last!!

Tara,

I am emailing you my thoughts because I'm both ashamed of my actions and feel that my best and most thorough expression is through written or typed words.

His name is Q, for Quentin. Five years ago, I met a young man named Q. We became friends instantly. After about a year and a half, we got back into contact after December of 2015. I couldn't have asked for a better friend.

As you know, the road of celibacy is no joke, not to mentioned being around the wrong people influencing your judgment and goals. I wasn't stable mentally, physically, or emotionally. In desperation to find peace somewhere, in someone, or even with something, I decided to turn my back on my health.

Every moment I felt less than. I constantly felt angry because I had to hate myself every step of the way to find this comfort. It was a comfort instilled in me at a young age- not even young, some would say a baby. I was soothing my soul tie, and as I was soothing it, I was worsening the connections I had developed so closely to my trauma and other people's demons. See, I was killing myself to destroy the soul tie I had with my cousins, to remove both of my grandfathers' hands, I was ripping away my clarity to dissimulate my mother leaving and how she birthed me through her constant battles with soul ties. I was tugging at my own soul in the attempt to fortify someone else's, because isn't it appropriate to sacrifice myself for the comfort of others? Because is it both astonishing and honorable to choose my own destruction- to be in charge of my own generosity?

This tie became my life. Everyone knew I couldn't focus around Q. I couldn't even breathe. I remember him telling me about a late rapper named XXXtentacion, who was murdered by another young rapper- some said he was controversial- I soon considered him relatable. So, because he listened, I did too. I connected as he did, and the obsession like his with music was like listening to him. So, I could only imagine the things he didn't say but that he heard.

As time goes on, I don't want to heal. The growth, the peace, the responsibility, it all makes too much sense. Therefore, I cannot thrive in peace because insanity is my home.

I'd try to maintain busy because it gives my mind more of an opportunity to greet him. I think about him most when I'm busiest. When I'm alone and calm, I'm in autopilot because that serenity didn't exist when I was with him.

What do you do when your mind lingers most when it is busy?

This may sound heart aching, but again, there is comfort in the pain I cause. To hurt is familiar, and to be honest, I just don't know what else to feel.

Therefore, I could not blame him for the warnings that I chose to ignore. I will not chastise him for my lack of obedience. But I cherish those few happy moments when I can shift my mind on all that I have imagined and the desires of my heart when the atmosphere permits me to completely neglect what I already know. So eventually, I no longer blamed him. I keep going back and forth because I'm still looking for him to say something that will make me want to stay. I keep crying because it's painful, laughing because it's familiar, and at the same time, I'm calm because I know better. But If I love someone, then I owe them my body, my money, my time, my heart, etc. I owe them everything precious I could ever give, so I keep going. I keep going because I hear this voice, and it keeps saying to dance with the devil, keep dancing, if it isn't working, keep dancing... it's working. Dance along to the pain, embrace incineration, fall for the insanity. Yes, I'm still falling for the insanity.

Two weeks later.

"Janee, I received your email," Tara said after a huge welcoming smile.

I returned her smile as I handed her a paper that read:

Tara,

I didn't know how many times I would say goodbye. So, I threw out my sheets, deleted the texts and photos. Any poem, any thought that reminded me of him. I scrubbed my body and cared for my dehydrated skin. I no longer wanted to feel him. I no longer wanted him a part of my body.

Annie said deliverance is a choice, and no matter how many times a day I thought of him, I would not contact him, I would not search for him or unblock him. I would constantly play his last truth: "Bitch, who would ever want you with your tendencies?" This didn't hurt my feelings. Instead, I instantly asked myself, "Who wouldn't?"

Sometimes to keep me going, I'd replay the fact that in order to get me back, he played with my faith. He went to church to please me, he lied and said he wanted to have a baby with me just to feel me and as he reposted a scripture on Facebook, he boldly said, "Y'all God." Which confirmed we do not have the same God. Q was someone I used to know back in 2014, 2015, 2016, and 2017. This Q is lost, this Q is healing, and this Q is not worthy of any attachment to me.

I love him forever and always, but I don't want him. I don't want him because I want myself instead.

"I am happy for you Janee," Tara said.

Later on that same month, I found myself emailing Tara once more:

Fool me once shame on you. Fool me twice, shame on me. Fool me again, what's wrong with me?

"God showed me a man standing behind you. I can't see his face, but I see you crying in sorrow. There is either a man coming or a man you haven't let go. This man is going to hurt you and have you questioning your worth. I see depression trying to creep back in. Be careful."—Daniel

According to Vocabulary.com, sorrow, /särō, 'sôrō/, is a feeling of deep sadness that is closely related to grief. This immense sadness can occur from disappointment, loss, and suffering. I had done it again, ran back to the very thing and situation that had broken me. I was falling, and I had to keep falling- I wanted to touch the ground badly. I thought by the time I hit the ground, I would feel nothing- I'd be numb. I'd lose myself and be fully engulfed by him. Him, the one who seemed to hardly want to deal with the love of my life; the reason for my existence: Jesus. We strengthened our soul tie and built a faulty foundation. As I poured into him, he drained me- there wasn't one moment I didn't feel insecure when I was with him. Maybe he would like this girl? Is this relationship a lie? I'd think about the countless times he had begged his way back into my life. I wondered if his statuses were about me. When he was pouring out his heart, I didn't know if it was to me. When he was persistent, I didn't know if it was to attract me. I just didn't know... I wondered how he truly felt about me. Did he see the light through me? Did I show him something different? Maybe we can be together? No, no, he CAN'T stay here. But please don't go. I had moved my heart's enemy and depression into my apartment. I began to hate that space- I never wanted to go home. Bumping my head repetitively! See, I was getting used to the rejection, the heartbreak, the errors, the setbacks. Insanity was starting to make sense again. I can't breathe...I can't breathe with him around- I trapped myself again.

Jesus's love is freedom. I can't wait to be free.

"So, what now, Janee?" Tara asked.

"I have to get up. The journey is too great," I said.

"I did my own assignment. Previously you asked me to touch on every relationship, but I didn't. Here are some 'new' secrets:"

"Men"

I recently watched a movie based on a woman pushing the importance of writing down all the things wanted in a man. I sat and thought for months-the funny thing is, I didn't know what I wanted. I don't know what that man looks like, how he would talk, his demeanor or anything. I didn't know what I wanted in a man.

Cordell

Cordell was a boy I went to high school with. He was in that classic class that everyone considered, the slow class. But the tripped-up thing about it was the kids weren't challenged, they just refused to do their work in an orderly fashion (I'm shocked I wasn't in there). I ignored him throughout high school because, like I previously expressed, I wasn't interested in black guys, let alone TALL men.

In an effort to forget about Q, I entertained Cordell. He was a low budget drug dealer, and nothing was popping in his life. He was a gloomy disaster. I always said that man would do anything but cuff me. Our song was, Let Me Ease Your Mind by Boosie, and my mind wasn't chaotic around him when that song was playing. My mind was dead. The more I thought about him, the more my spirit was vexed. Of all the options in the world, he chose this life. I tried to force myself to accept him, but I could never accept the fact that someone like him sold drugs to my biological mother, and that's why I had to go into foster care. That's why people that weren't good to me had access to me. Drugs ruined my childhood; someone laced my father's weed and made him schizophrenic. So, the nerve I had sitting there, trying to form any relationship with him, and sleeping with him. Letting him touch me was an insult to me and my healing.

I remembered Mel's reaction when she found out I had sex with him. "Janee, you're having sex with that man! Are you ok?" she was concerned. All of this was a slap in the face to myself and all that I had been through. What he did disgust me, it wasn't fun, and I didn't find it cute. He was ruining lives, ruining families, and his occupation had caused me much pain in my life, all because he desired to "supply the demand." I would never accept him.

I remember I tried to force the demons to stay inside of me. I downed that vodka smooth and pressed on to someone that didn't care to relieve me. I remember the darkness I carried around me and crying to anything to come free me. I wallowed to Camille, to Auntie Candace, and I even tried reaching God, but I couldn't hear him. The next night I had to escape from my health for one minute. I had to meet an appointment with insanity, because at that moment, months free of self-harm wasn't comforting to me. I had to feel my old happiness again. After our meeting, I grabbed a shot of bleach, a few drops of Listerine, mixed in with some pills, and cheered with my demons. Eventually, I broke away after questioning constant yeast infections and an unforgettable statement. Every time I heard or saw his name, all I could hear was, "Bitch, you got all that shit on your arm, looking crazy. So, what if I sell crack. You're more of a liability than me."

You have heard too much about the other guys, so I decided to tie it all in, as you suggested. What's for me will find me. As I love myself, others that feel the same with gravitate to me, blah, blah, BLAH- all the things I know. Here's what I concocted: there is a common denominator between all these men, besides my vagina, haha—sexual abuse. I cannot count how many stories I have heard. Rico, Esha's cousin, was the worst. When he was between the ages of nine and 10, these two girls in their late teens doped him out with codeine and made him perform oral sex on them. When Q was a kid, some older ladies felt him up, and he's still healing to this day. Cordell's teenage babysitter molested him, and that's where his love for BBWs (Big Black Women) stemmed from. When Chris was little, a man tried to rape him and attempted to make him have sex with another boy while filming it. I watched Chris's soul leave his body as he replayed it in his mind while explaining it all to me. I was dealing with broken men, and while dealing with each one of them, we were trading our darkness while I was trying to heal them. And I was too fond of toxicity; it still helps sleep at night. I still look for it in men, and I still scrub my skin after every encounter. I think the pain that they projected onto me was healing them. And as far as being a good woman, you know a "ride or die," I just want to know if I'm rare or stupid.

I kept it up with Q for so long because my soul seemed to summon him when comfort was needed the most. I had to get out on that chilly October day. I had to feel that cold love again because I loved the chill.

Had to revisit the song.

Had to watch the movies and shows repeatedly.

I even found the theme songs.

I had to feel the pain again.

But I'll continue to avoid the numbness. I'm starting to feel nearly every day now.

—Janee

"Wow," Tara said. "Anything else you have to amaze me with?"

"Yes, I attempted to create a message," I said.

"A message?" she asked.

"I have been doing some self-cleaning and thought it'd be beneficial to teach others and inform them of the acknowledgment and wisdom God has blessed me with," I answered.

"This ought to be good, dear. You're an excellent writer," she said. "I love this new homework you have made for yourself."

I cleared my throat.

"For Those That Need to Be Needed"

Janee S. Dukes

"Dear God, dear loving, heavenly Father,

I come to You humbly with elation and gratefulness for this message You have gifted me. Let it encourage, uplift, and connect with someone. Glory to God, you are worthy. I love You, infinitely. Amen."—JSD

Ephesians 2:10—

"For we are his workmanship, created in Christ Jesus unto good works, which God hath before ordained that we should walk in them."

What feelings have you gotten yourself in lately? Yes, you. We know that one of the biggest enemies of this world is our mind. What we feed it, who we engage with, what and who we connect it with, and how we handle our minds. Often, we are encouraged to follow our hearts when faced with difficult decisions. The Bible says to 'guard our hearts, for everything we do flows from it' (i.e., Proverbs 24:3). But what do we do when our heart misleads us? What happens when we make people, our desires, our feelings, etc. our God(s)?

Some of us even make ourselves our own God! We take credit for God's work—we fall in love with being needed.

If you are anything like me, a few of my best qualities include:

- Compassion
- Humor
- Resilience
- Tenacity
- Creativity
- Intelligence
- Wit
- Wisdom

Out of the few "positive" qualities, the majority of them relate to others or are presumed a quality. What are your God-given qualities? At times we may feel as though those priceless qualities are not enough. It's not enough to be brave, smart, or funny. To some, these qualities are not apparent because we don't have the courage to act solely on them to have a permanent effect on people. Instead, we engulf ourselves and others into tangible things. We buy our way into acceptance, relationships, occupations, pleasure, friendships, "happiness," and some even attempt to buy their way into a relationship with God.

People "buy" their way through life, not knowing who they are, not standing, and acknowledging their God-given qualities- they simply aren't enough. This possibly comes from a weak foundation with God. Not knowing our place and who we are in God breeds envy, jealousy, loneliness, and low self-esteem. Thus we seek negative gratification through being needed. When this occurs, we lose sight of what matters the most- edifying God. Some of us consider ourselves the glue that holds everything together in our lives, whether personal or professional. But what happens when people become their own glue? What happens when the dust settles? We feel the weakness of not being needed. We lose sight of our purpose and make this challenge and victory about us. If you need to feel needed, then who is your God?

Man has an egregious habit of forgetting God. Whether we are letting our faith waver, or bask in the excitement of a new blessing and neglect to give God what is due to Him. Glory to Him can be easily lost when money, fame, intelligence, and other factors are involved. We may get lost in the absence of thank yous and have ill feelings when we aren't noticed. Seeking that gratification, we make ourselves accessible to trouble by pouring from an empty cup without God's guidance. And because of that need to be needed, we tend to push what God has commanded of us to the side. Is seeking gratification, curing loneliness, buying love and happiness affecting what God has instructed you to do for His glory?

Be transparent: if you were/are anything like me, then you may recognize the need to be needed. Growing up, I was needed for various things, pleasures, and to comfort others. But essentially, it all made me extremely uncomfortable. Risking and offering my discomfort for others was natural for me. If I wasn't in some type of despair, the world seemed unbearable to me. I sacrificed my value for others and willingly fell into a complete obligation for any and everyone who showed me an ounce of love. Not knowing my place in God had poisoned me with the need of being needed- I had made people my God.

God knows us, and He knows our purpose. Because He knows us, there is no need to be needed. Ephesians 2:10 states, "For we are his workmanship, created in Christ Jesus unto good works, which God hath before ordained that we should walk in them." There is no "I" in the heart the Lord has given us. An "I" should not exist even when God uses our hands to bless and uplift or encourage others. His mercy, grace, and glory should be in our hearts, and that should fulfill us- not the "I's, we's or me's" that may poison our minds and deflect us from His purpose. Galatians 2:20, "I am crucified with Christ: nevertheless I live; yet not I, but Christ liveth in me: and the life which I now live in the flesh I live by the faith of the Son of God, who loved me, and gave himself for me." Our hearts are treacherous, and our minds can be misleading. Let us not walk in our own gratification of doing for others, it is easy to buy our "comfortability" and deem it genuine, but in 1 Corinthians 3:20, God says, "Our work will be shown for what it is— And again, The Lord knoweth the thoughts of the wise, that they are vain". I trust it's better to follow God's footsteps, which assures we are not led astray.

Therefore, rejoice when the Lord trusts you with His people- rejoice in that opportunity to give God all the glory and resist the temptation of feeling needed because the only need in this world is the Lord. He gifted us hands, a heart, willingness, and personal yet special qualities. He saw us fit to aid Him in carrying out His mission. What a joy it is to know that God found us fit to yearn for Him, glorify Him and solely need Him. Be grateful that the Lord loves you, likes you, finds value in you, knows your worth, and accepts you. Rejoice because you will NEVER have to buy, force your way, belittle your way, or manipulate your way into His arms. God is who is needed; God is all that is needed.

Tara, tearing up, asked, “How do you feel, Janee?”

“I feel free. I have surrendered to the Lord,” I said. “I am now finally free.”

Chapter Thirteen

MORNING GLORY

I looked in the mirror today and nearly fell out. The first thing my mind yelled was that I am beautiful. I had gained something special, something priceless. I will never forget what occurred two weeks ago. A gay white man (that part is important because gay men never lie nor do young children) from Emory college once said to me at a gala that my scholarship foundation hosts yearly, "You look beautiful. Don't ever settle. I'm gay, and you know we keep it real. Don't you ever settle."

Another gay white man at the gala said to me, "My God, look at you!" Rubbing my dress, he continued, "This and this. You look so beautiful. This dress is like none other- so elegant, so elegant."

At my gala table, there were two women in white dresses. They were beautiful, but I had already made up in my mind that they were jump offs. I didn't give them the respect to ask them where they were from or what they did. My peers and I just sat silently, making faces to each other one way while smiling in their faces the other way.

Those were the only women guests that went out their way to be kind to us. They danced with us. They told me, "Black girls f-ing rock. You are beautiful. Look at your dress- we've been talking about it all night. You are beautiful. F what they say. If you ever need hair or make-up, reach out to us. If we are not available, we will find someone who is." And they embraced me over and over as I cried because they were so nice, and my thoughts and facial expressions were so mean. But it didn't take me long to do a self-assessment. This insecurity, this illness I had both because of the seeds planted and my thoughts watering them, was toxic.

I met a girl that same weekend I attended the gala. She didn't care about what others thought of her. She was so kind to everyone. She had the highest GPA of all the graduates at the gala and was the one with the best spirit. I clung to her because she was what I wanted to be: free. From that day on, I decided to live for God and me.

Shortly after, I cried out to God. I cried for confidence, and I cried for peace with my confidence so I could proceed in my success. I owned up to the obstacles I had created and God did it right there! From that night on, I held my head high. I took pride in my attire, I smiled at everyone, and I loved me. I loved me on the days I didn't feel like it, while tears were rolling down my face. And as they rolled down, I found peace and joy. Peace and joy because I could feel the girl I used to know escape me, I felt the devil tremble in his tracks every time I shouted, "JESUS, JESUS!" And I was even more elated and fulfilled because I knew that my love for others would only increase. Then I had to think about my creation, the life God gifted me:

My rebirth shined so brightly. I unraveled and bloomed into something unforgettable, something undefined. Tough times caused me to tense up, like the petals of a morning glory. I am clothed in strength, and like the roots of the flower, I am thick and unbreakable. I can grow in the roughest and most toxic situations and conquer all the wars that occur in the depths of the thickest soil. My stem grows tall, to see beyond what's not meant to be seen. My cognizance grows in cold climates. I provide shade for the weak. Though my strong coating can be poisonous- invading people's minds and attacking their weaknesses. Sometimes I smother and pollute other plants. But every morning is a new bloom, a new kind of beauty. My seeds of wisdom plant and spread throughout different lives. My representation of glory is continuously blossoming with honor and astonishing beauty. Growing constantly into something, someone who can't be more brilliant or less defined by luminosity, but never higher or brighter than the light of God.

As I literally dust myself off, I close my eyes and inwardly thank Tara for all she has done. I give her a big hug and hold on for as long as I can. When

I open my eyes and look in the mirror, I see me holding myself. There is not one earthly person who can take the credit for all that God has done for me. I thank Him for working through me and allowing me to be a vessel for others and in my own life. He couldn't have sent me a better Tara than myself. He worked through my conscious and made me a whole other person. Until my mind demands again, thank you, Tara.

The Harvest.

God will give you a platform to use to bring young people to Christ. Your life is that testimony. And because of what has been instilled in you, you are a mighty weapon. You are a threat to the enemy because you can take back the young people that he has claimed.

"All stand for the honorable Judge Janee Dukes," the bailiff commanded.

Walking up to the bench, I noticed a teenage girl with her head bowed, refusing to stand, "You may be seated," I called.

"Calling case number 56781, in the 2011 case of D'Mya Smith," the courtroom clerk called.

I see the same girl approach with four people beside her. "State your names please," I said.

"Good morning Judge, I am Carol Chaney reporting from the Oakland county DHHS office of Michigan."

"Hello Judge, I am Francesca Michael, an Oakland County caseworker at Judith Charities."

"Hi, your Honor, I am Catherine Stokes, a prosecutor of Oakland County Michigan stationed at this court."

"Morning, Judge Dukes, my name is Jim Thompson, case attorney for Ms. Smith and her father."

I nodded my head at each one and glanced at the youth. She fidgeted a little.

"Oh, hi. I am D'Mya Smith," she said.

I smiled at her.

"What is the reason for your appearance today?" I asked.

"Well Judge, D'Mya is seventeen years old. She was formerly placed in Southgate, Michigan with her half-brother's great Aunt, Karen Clyde, for almost two years," Francesca stated.

"Well, what happened?" I questioned, looking around for an answer.

Catherine starts, "Judge, D'Mya has had excessive behavior problems over the years. Over twenty suspensions in her school career and behavioral problems at home." I glanced again at the youth. "She was caught bleaching her brother's belongings after the two had a disagreement," she said.

"What does her file say? Any issues at her previous homes?" I asked, eager to be informed.

"There are questionable cases as to whether D'Mya was sexually abused by different family members and family associates, two including her grandfathers on both her mother's and father's side of the family. Physical and mental abuse by her great grandmother and great uncle on her father's side. Her father was also diagnosed with paranoia schizophrenia almost a decade ago," Jim stated.

"Note that these are all questionable accusations," Catherine added.

"D'Mya, I would like to hear from you," I said.

She just continued to bow her head; I imagined the tears preparing to roll down her face.

"D'Mya, may I tell you about a girl I used to know?" I asked.

BIBLICAL MESSAGES

All biblical messages were presented by my father, Gabriel M. McCullum, my sister Kiara A. Johns, my mother April McCullum, or myself unless otherwise specified.

Dad,

I just wanted to let you know that I listen to you and I hear you. I am remembering and praising God as He uses you and has used you, to connect the dots in my life. Everything spoken has aligned with my life, every note I've taken I have looked back on and kept with me and shared. I thank God for you.

THE HALL OF FAME

Thank you, Gabriel, and April McCullum for the lifelong seeds that you both planted in me in this season, and the seasons that will come to pass. It seemed impossible to find a forever until I met my family. Unconditional love couldn't have a better example than you two. God couldn't have chosen better parents. My angels: God outdid himself when he created you both.

Special thanks to Saba Gebrai. I will never forget your kind words, "When they look in the dictionary for resilience, they will see your name." Anyone that has ever had contact with you has called you an angel. Thank you deeply and wholeheartedly for your heart and undying support.

Kiara A. Johns, Tiana L. Nelson, Ke'Lan Foard, and Jay'Vone J. McCullum, thank you for opening your arms to several girls in need. For quickly and genuinely accepting us all into your family; as your siblings. Thank you for sharing pieces of the best parts of you all; your parents and your heart(s).

Thank you, Kristina Avant-Mays, "You are brilliant," beams throughout my heart during times that I feel limited. You are forever my Auntie Krissy, and I am quick to choose quality over quantity because of you!

Thank you, Deianne Lacey. I never understood your teachings- they confused me and made me upset. But my heart couldn't help but to gravitate towards you and love you. The confusion, hesitation, and discussions have grown an overwhelming certainty in my life.

Thank you, Joyce Murphy, my auntie, for your patience, heart, understanding, and obedience to God. Thank you ever so much for listening to God when He had you reveal my purpose.

Thank you, Cherelle McGhee, although you have no intention of hanging out with me, so Auntie is befitting, Carrie Joseph, Carol Garibaldi, my BEST friend and sister Khaleya Spence, and all my other past and current mentors, social workers, friends, but most importantly family.

To my Papa, Michael James Smith. I always wondered what my life would've been like if you were still here. I now understand why you couldn't be; I hope you are proud; I love you.

I love you all indefinitely.

Made in the USA
Monee, IL
06 April 2021

63994804R00089